THE
DISCOMBOBULATED
ALPHA

THE DISCOMBOBULATED ALPHA

A True Story

THE
DISCOMBOBULATED
ALPHA

BY CRAIG 'BOB' AINSWORTH

Contents

Introduction

LIFE IS AN ADVENTURE, ACT ACCORDINGLY!

I am a veteran Royal Marine Commando, elite bodyguard, and Interpol associate. I know, sexy line, right? Well, I can assure you the reality is far from a manicured James Bond highlight reel full of fast cars, choreographed violence, and where the good guys always win.

To me, that line encapsulates my evolution from a bullied London lad immersed in a culture of mediocrity. Through seemingly endless humbling's, battles with imposter syndrome, perfectionism, my discombobulated ego, and a plethora of enlightening life lessons masquerading as unconquerable adversities. I loved every second of it. My journey took me all over the world, to world's most will never see. Introducing myself to elite mindsets most will unfortunately never know, and horrific truths I hope most never learn; believe me ignorance is often blissful compared to truth, but hard truths soon became my business.

Growing up in North London will expose a man to many things that teach him the ultimate price of victor or victim. I thought I knew it all. I went through a little bit of tragedy and felt to the world owing me something for my grief and suffering. It did not. However, this entitled attitude would soon be banished from my mind forever after having the honour of spending priceless hours immersed in the world of the 0.01%, The Royal Marines, and the 0.0001%, Billionaires; two very different worlds that taught me everything I am today. I feel extremely grateful to have had the opportunity to learn from a glorious cocktail of strong women, gangsters, elite soldiers, eclectic Billionaire's, and visionary's that taught me that anything is possible when you truly believe in yourself. Inspired! I mean, I protected a plethora of legends like the Ben Affleck, Gal Gadot, Henry Cavil, Jason Momoa, F. Gary Gray, Chris Hemsworth, Tessa Thompson, Zendaya, Tom Holland, Eddie Redmayne, Scorsese, Pacino, De Niro, and Johnny Depp; to name a few. Plus, a horde of Government officials, so-called dignitaries, and an array of Royalty and elites. It has also been alleged that I supported global operations to capture high profile targets in joint cross-border operations on behalf of Interpol and her partners. Real "Bond" shit.

Cocooned in this world of excellence I became conditioned to the culture of success. Adopting a growth mindset based upon extreme ownership, accountabilities, pragmatism, and belief systems that evolved my mentality; removing self and replacing it with an obsession to become the best version of myself. I began despising my old lazy, stupid self the more I levelled up. Leaving friends and family behind as I became allergic to bullshit mediocrity and excuses.

Normalising this mentality taught me the biggest lesson of my life; that we are all our biggest hero and villain. Capable of achieving our wildest dreams, overcoming unconquerable adversities, or manifesting our biggest nightmares. The divider, having the courage and accountability to get to know your true self so you can reflect honestly and provide yourself with the chance to build the desired version of yourself. You can't start a race if you don't know where the starting line is can you? But unlike any other project in your life, this is a 100% solo mission where we must be brutal, yet lovingly honest with ourselves. Focusing all our energy on the things we can change, like our habits and rituals; however, humans are funny creatures and despite us all knowing what is good for us, we each make mistakes and more often than not, fail to practice what we preach. But that's ok, accept it and own it, we are all human, but the real superpower is knowing your true self. Public bullshit removed, we must always hold onto the essence of who we are or risk losing ourselves to the madness of life. Remembering that the juice must always be worth the squeeze or risk becoming bitter!

Belief in oneself and knowing who you are is the foundation to everything great. Sounds simple, right? It's not. In fact, it is one of the rarest characteristics of a person in today's societies as we are held to ransom and oppressed by manicured ignorance, such as cancel-culture and an out-of-control tyrannical media agenda designed to divide us with fear of other; each other. A minefield of political correctness gone mad and an inhuman set of unachievable standards that has not only alienated us from each other, but far worse, alienated us from our true selves!

Lost in a labyrinth of fear, identity and marketed desires sent to our phones that listen to our conversations with friends or colleagues, many of us become so lost in the world's idea of us that we give up on our own. However, every great that ever lived, every legend, inventor, genius, or great leader has fought off cultural and social constraints to blaze their own path based upon seemingly deluded self-belief and their ability to achieve their goal. They believed in themselves despite the adversities they faced because they knew something others didn't, they had a plan and executed it whilst remaining flexible enough to adapt and overcome along the way. You can too! I promise that you are capable of becoming anything in life, but you need to commit. It is you who must change, the world will not change for you or anybody else and will be the same after you evolve only you will not recognize it. You are all capable of becoming a version of yourself you can't even begin to imagine; believe me, if I can achieve what I have, you can achieve anything! I will prove it to you as I we go through my journey in sometimes humiliating detail.

Manifestation is an inside job. A process of self-belief. We need to believe so deeply in our ability to grow into the person capable of achieving our goal or overcoming our adversity that we seek accountability and actively work to adopt the characteristics and lessons needed to transform ourselves. Most people manifest through desperation. Waiting until the last possible moment and hour of need to force them out of choice and into a situation of necessity. Others are put in situations, even born into them, where there is no choice but to act. Forced to sink or swim. I am one of those people. That's why I have always idolized rags to riches stories and those who have started with nothing but ended with everything those who started well above them could only dream of levitating to. I am nothing if not a romantic dreamer. Appreciating the hard work and dedication others have achieved to become great is something that taught me tolerance and understanding as I recognized from a young age that no matter who you are or where you're from, you can become the master of your own destiny. Accountability being the initiator, discipline the engine. Knowing, knowing! I'm not as good as those around me, but that I could be if I focus is one of the biggest lessons I have learnt. I only wish someone had slapped that into me as a kid. Literally. But the secret to life is not so secret, I just wasn't listening. As many of you will not listen now.

I was 100% effort and fearless, but with zero direction or self-belief; expecting results because I tried really-really hard. But results are earned, not negotiated. Like I said, we often know what's best for us but do not act on it, misled by our ego and fear. But life doesn't give a fuck and there are no participation medals in the real world, just winners and losers. Today, those who dedicate themselves to the battle within, there is more opportunity than any other time in human history. We are all fighting two wars, internal and external, so let's all hold fire on attacking each other's external as much as humanly possible and seek our own truth over other imperfections of others and become the best versions of ourselves. For us first; everyone else a firm second.

To be empowered is to be open and vulnerable to the possibility of growth and lessons from all around us. Composed and secure in our own self-valuation, yet constantly seeking new ideas and belief systems to challenge it instead of wasting our energy on others egos and fears in a self-destructive cycle of toxicity. This mindlessness of doing the same thing over and over again whilst expecting a different result is the literal definition of insanity. Yet, people do it every day, caught in the conundrum of being equally fearful and obsessed with the unknown as they are their current situations but are frozen in fearful indecision. The choice of being a product of your environment or evolving from it is a defining one, and one we must revisit constantly in our lives if we are to maintain a what we achieve. Others are feared but we must embrace it to be our best selves. Think about how often people in the public eye reinvent themselves to stay relevant. Well this is your story and your relevance is your choice, as is the choice to peruse it.

I grew up in the world's most multicultural city, where rich and poor live side by side, emersed in diversity. I had the blessing to learn from so many diverse cultures, perceptions, values, rituals, and ideas; many conflicting but all priceless in forming my tolerances that enabled me to excel later in life. Empowering me to "fit-in" with such legends and professionals, achieving so much so quickly because I had the gift of knowing that geniuses learn from everyone and everything. I recognized early in my life that there are many kinds of success and genius. Everyone I grew up with was so different, same-same but different. I learnt very early on that where you're your history does not define your destiny and the only limitations are the ones, we put on ourselves. I was raised to accept loss, not learn from it. I was raised to accept being dumber, slower, lesser, poorer, to just do my best… But never how to be brave enough to take accountability and become better or successful, so I had to go out into the world hunting for that mindset and tribe that would lead me to the path leading to where I wanted to go, and who I wanted to be. I learnt to never judge and always look for the lesson. This is why I became unstoppable in my pursuit of success. How can anyone fail when they are awake and willing to learn from everyone and everything? You can't, it is only a matter of time.

I am going to walk you through how a mediocre terrified kid destined for a life of silent desperation and participation medals learnt from his losses and unceremoniously suffered through the necessary growth to become an elite soldier and travelled the world with celebrities, experiencing lavish wealth and secret societies you wouldn't believe even if I showed you.

Before 2020 my life was full of adventure, purpose and all the success I had set out to achieve, and more. But I had fallen in love with the process and the purpose my work had offered me. Keeping me busy, challenged and surrounded by elite mindsets and impressive people that ensured I was a little fish in an ocean of iron I could sharpen mine against. Suddenly! Tragedy struck the world, and we were all sent home and told to stay there. Aware of what was coming as the tactics were so blatant, I began to spiral as I bounced around my lovely Surrey home and climbed the walls without an outlet to keep my mind from remembering. Then, after losing 11 friends in 16 months, I fell into a deep depression. I had been deteriorating mentally for years in civilian life as I began drowning in other's victimhood and selfish mindsets that were now so alien to me. I craved the challenge and mourned the loss of iron to keep me sharp. I felt although I were mourning my dreams and the life I once had. I craved the truth and challenge that had seemingly vanished since I took the role as head of security for Fantastic Beasts. The pursuit of excellence had been exchanged for babysitting corruption, selfishness, and emotionally led entitlement with no rational or factual relevance for my pragmatic mindset to gain traction. I don't expect you to understand at this point because I had money, a lovely Surrey home, brand new Mercedes, every woman I ever wanted; but I had lost everything I needed in life. True purpose. With one finger looming over the self-destruct button, I started to self-sabotage. Grief and heartbreak made me weak enough to allow my long lost demons back in, and I welcomed them with open arms. I began slipping deeper and deeper into the darkness until one day I went for a stroll in Richmond Park to take my own life. Almost in protest that no one else had managed to.

I had witnessed so many who had everything, but felt they had nothing; like them I became lost in the ridiculousness of life until the solitude of Covid sent me on a horrific yet much-needed journey of hellish rediscovery that nearly killed me.

I had fallen so far but realized only I could save myself. I began tearing at the layers of chameleon I had adopted throughout my life, obsessing over my mistakes, personal fuckery, successes, and everything I could control; and could not.

I began obsessively writing everything down. I started to gain traction. Literally teaching myself about myself and building momentum with renewed confidence. After writing a new TV show and having the opportunity to speak with a two-time Emmy winning Producer. I was buzzing! A new life, the one I always wanted, my dream!

Then life reminded me that it had its own plans whilst we are busy making our own. The very next day after selling the idea. I received a WhatsApp to say my brother from another had passed away. I had messaged him the night before to tell him about my TV show – eventually messaging him asking, 'you alive brother?'. He wasn't. I fell apart. Fury and guilt filling my veins. I wasn't fucking there again! The loss and crippling sadness overwhelmed me as childhood tragedy flooded back memories of my best friend being murdered when I was 17. Both my friends had the same name and a son on the way, it was just too much. It felt like a personal punishment. I mean how self-absorbed does that sound, but it's the truth and how I felt in my grief. Such pain sent me on a desperate mission to rationalize and understand. It seems insane to even be writing this but that's how I felt at the time. Tragically, many never get a chance, but this event opened my emotional floodgates, and it didn't disappoint. It was nothing short of a biblical flood. Years of buried emotions flooded back and overwhelmed me. I am only here today because a couple of genuine Royal Marine brothers came to save me from me at a moment's notice. They gripped me and put me back together; reminding me who I was. Pulled me out of bed, from ledges and made sure someone was with me. I will be eternally grateful and owe a debt to the world, hence why I am writing this book. Demanded by the lads who helped me in my hour.

I went to a fucking horrible, dark, and scary place, where there was no joy, gratitude, desire or even time: and it wasn't for the Royal Marine Brotherhood stepping in to save my self-destructing self from... well, myself. I wouldn't be sat here awkwardly writing this today.

Former Royal Marine Commando and Atlantic Rower, Juniour, dropped everything to move in with me for three months. Helping me regain some gratitude and perspective whilst on epic hikes and daily walks in nature and farmlands with my two French Bulldogs, Lilo & Stitch. It was in these moments away from technology, obligations and even my enslaving ambition that I was able to start a new journey, building a roadmap to the person I now wanted to become.

Whilst on these walks I decided to write this book because not only did it give me purpose, but if I can help just one person out there to realise that the person they are so desperately searching for to save them is already within and waiting to be unleashed, then it would all be worth it.

Despite how cliché or cheesy it maybe, we are all capable of such wonders and all our own biggest hero and villain. It was time to remind myself of this fact.

I had the honour of operating with and working for the world's elite. Everyone is inspirational in their individual pursuit of excellence with consistent efforts to maintain, learn and grow, in that order. Continuously revaluating their approach and evolving in real time to remain flexible and adaptable to any opportunity that might arise. This requires a cocktail of insane self-belief and self-awareness.

Alphas live among every demographic; I have seen it with my own two blues. I operated with a female medic in her twenties who was attached to our Commando multiple in Helmand Province, Afghanistan. She was an absolute warrior and 'one of the lads'; I have met Zulu tribesmen who became Hollywood film crew, female Apache helicopter pilots, a modern-day slave who escaped Africa to become a chauffeur for celebrities on huge blockbuster movies. A Venezuelan sexual assault victim who became a loving wife, mother, and activist for men's mental health to stop the cycle of abuse she had experienced so brutally; and a scroll of other legends that the word inspiration doesn't quite cover. Each overcoming unimaginable adversities to change their stars and make the world a better place, whilst setting an incredible example for all those who have the honour to meet them or hear their stories, even if told through aliases. The world can never have enough genuine inspiration and we all need a daily dose, I know I do.

The number one lesson I learnt from these crazy experiences is that we are all human and the most impressive people and stories are far from the lights of Hollywood or a privileged silver spoon upbringing, because character is simply not built-in ivory towers but in the trenches of adversity. The most impressive people I have met are the silent heroes who fall nine times but get up ten; those who become the hero of their own life, and the truly enlightened who spend their lives dedicated to others. It is here that I found my inspiration and feel so blessed to have witnessed it as their examples have helped inspire me in my own life and keep my ego in check when I feel the world is against me.

Sitting with Junior, Lilo & Stitch in my house one day, feeling very sorry for myself, I knew I needed to get my shit together. I had wallowed long enough and if I wasn't going to get busy dying, I needed to get busy living. Talking with Junior about our experiences and lives in general helped me regain focus through gratitude and self-belief, and over time our conversations turned to how we could share this with the world. Junior was blown up whilst travelling in a mastiff deep in Helman province, Afghanistan. He had been on a journey of recovery that gave me perspective on my own suffering, but together we spoke of a deep desire to help others gain perspective on their own lives and learn from our sufferings and life lessons without having to go through the experiences themselves. Especially Juniors. I call this Safari Learning. Being able to learn from intense situations and painful lessons without the suffering or threat of violence. This provides opportunity via hindsight and allows us to learn through these simulated experiences. Much like training for war with the Royal Marines. Or an actor rehearsing... it's a mind set and headspace we can train ourselves to adopt until it becomes automatic.

Your life is your responsibility and I genuinely feel obligated to share my lessons with you so I can prove that you can become a level of yourself you have not even begun to imagine but you do not foresee a possible process.

This book is in line with all 183 NDA's (Non-Disclosure Agreements) and one hell of a 50-year NDA I have signed over the years. I will in no way violate the people's privacy or trust in who I have served and protected, let me make that clear. I will simply be telling my story and the lessons I have learnt along the way, with names and locations changed to protect those who enabled me to walk this path and become the person I am today. Love, loyalty, and time are all we have, everything else is a beautiful bouquet of bullshit.

Remember that everything you see has been manifested by us humans. In security my role was simply to protect people from people; security is people protecting people from people, nothing more. The Discombobulated Alpha is about the humanity behind the wars, glamour, and adversities, instead of the usual salacious gossip. The truth is far more entertaining than lies when told in its truest form, from the wall of each side's argument, told by the man in the middle. The opinions in this book are my own and reflect my perception of everything I have witnessed along the way, but all stories and facts expressed as such can be proven... as I have said, the truth is always spicier than lies.

Here is my story...

Disclaimer:
All the following is alleged, with names, dates and locations changed to protect those involved.

Chapter 1

YOUR HISTORY DOES NOT
DEFINE YOUR DESTINY

I grew up in sunny North London with my parents and two younger siblings. We weren't broke-broke, but we never had the money for the luxuries everyone else seemed to have around us. I barely noticed unless someone else commented as I was an outdoors kid and forever in the woods on my bike. Enfield used to be the Kings hunting ground, but it belonged to me and my friends as we fantasized and built tree houses at every opportunity; you know, the old school shit kids don't seem to do anymore. Enfield was rough but as my brothers and I grew up it got naughtier and naughtier until we began to get caught up in it all. The little situations young men seem to at that age. I hated school and the whole conforming / tribalism that an all-Boys school can bring, so I spent most of my time out of school, uninterested and alone over the woods or at another school. I was always picked on or challenged because I was loud, unconforming and had developed a foul mouth and quick wit harnessed from a combative home and school life. The cycle was real, and I couldn't help myself. I was completely miserable and lonely and developed an anxious stutter as I second guessed my every word and action. Being bullied built callouses that still serve and hinder me to this day. Three little bastards used to wait for me every day after primary school. A local secondary school used to finish an hour earlier than my primary school so they would turn up with snacks and stuff to embarrass me with in front of my friends until no one would hang out with me through fear of getting the same treatment. I get it, but kids can be terrible, and this treatment drove me to solitude. I would spend my time with my 36 Guineapigs, 5 rabbits, or with my birds in an Avery my dad built had me in my bedroom. Safe and away from judgement I became truly introverted and spent all my time in my loft converted bedroom, hiding from projected anxieties downstairs and bullies outside. I was always alone and found it hard to integrate. I was loud and awkward, and most of my childhood memories are made up of feeling terrified and humiliated, like many, but this is my story and understanding that this is vital to the foundation of my story.

When I was little, I acted in a school play, The Owl and the Pussy Cat. I played the pig and when I walked out on stage everyone laughed on cue, but as I was so sensitive and unsupported, I fell to bits and cried myself off stage thinking this room of adults were laughing at me. My acting career was over before it started.

This set the tone for me, and I became introverted, stumbling over myself as I tried too hard to be liked by their kids and to fit in. I began playing football and my dad was

16

my manager. He spent most the time screaming at me and I could barely touch the ball without my anxiety trying to burst through my chest. I was shit until I got angry but when I did I would often score the winning goal or become a totally different player. A lesson of things to come.

One day we were watching the old Naked Gun movie with my dad where there is a scene that depicts sex between the two main characters with visuals of trains entering tunnels and other hilarious scenes. My dad was laughing out loud, I didn't get it and was openly frustrated, so my mum asked my dad, "is it time for the talk?". My father took me upstairs and asked me how I thought babies were made? Being the Guinea-pig expert, I boldly confessed to knowing that babies were made by males spitting into the female. My father cried with laughter before correcting his horrified son. A lovely heart-warming father son moment... destroyed by the fact he told my entire football team the following day. Adding unbearable embarrassment to my already lonely existence. Looking back, it was here I knew I was alone and think it's here I began to feel angry and bitter as I couldn't understand why everyone hated me so much. A victim mentality but one that would serve me as I found strength in solitude. Not giving a fuck what others think really is a superpower. My football drastically improved after this as my anger helped me focus. Burning through others' opinions as I learnt that if I couldn't join them, I could most certainly beat them.

I was part of a very successful school and domestic team and won several trophies, scoring the winning goals in a couple of finals and league games but I was doing it out of spite. I was competing with others and becoming bitter. This created a huge self-sabotaging mentality within my young, discombobulated brain, but ironically helped me overcome my bullies as I began to fight the fear and fight back. Like every bully, they soon left me alone, but little did they know my momentum had only just begun. Freedom and power are both addictive.

Life went on and I grew addicted to the safety of solitude. Spending most of my time alone or hidden away with my animals like the wonderful little weirdo I was. I wasn't interested in fitting in and saw others' desperation to do so as weakness. Looking back, I think this was because I had already spent so much time alone that I knew who I was, good and bad and was comfortable with it. I had the mentality from a young age that if others didn't like me, fuck them, that was their issue. If you are always looking to lease everyone in this way you end up not pleasing anyone. Especially yourself.

My father left when I was 15, I stepped up as man of the house as my mum needed a lot of support just figuring out standard things like getting her own car insurance and all the little things my father had managed for them both; these times were shit for everyone involved. Mum and I became a little team. She would work and I would play mum. At 15, and dealing with my own issues, and there were a lot, this dynamic shift not only affected me but my relationship with my mother and brothers forever. I was cast out of the sibling group; everything changed, and the amount of accountability and reliability required of me became immediately intense. My mother was an absolute legend, she raised three boys from 15, 11 and 9 years old with such grace and strength, it was amazing. She set an example of what a true alpha is, although I obviously saw the unfiltered version away from my brothers, she remains an absolute idol of mine during these times. Breakups are more common than not, but everything that was going on was alien at the time and I can only imagine at the age of 9 & 11, understanding why or what was going on must have been even more brutal. I saw the breakup coming as I was that little bit older and witnessed the conflicts, so it was almost a bit of a relief. I thought my mother would find herself a nice rich man to solve our problems, or at least someone to make her happy. My father's new girlfriend was just 25, 10 years older than me, so this cut my mum deep, even if she would never admit it. I didn't really realise at the time, but I quickly become numb to it all as I had to be strong for my mum, but looking back I was so isolated and genuinely started to hate the world and wonder why others seemed to have these perfect lives as mine fell to shit. Of course, everyone has problems, but you couldn't tell me this at 15.

We had negative money, and my job was to make sure we had no stress at home, so the boys were good at the game we created, the crime is getting caught. Despite my efforts to be a good son inside the house, I would let loose every chance outside of it.

I began to get a reputation, not as a hard man or someone to be feared, but as someone you should just leave alone. Bouncing around the pubs of Enfield at fifteen hanging out with older lads and chasing older girls, you often get yourself into older problems. I was exposed to too much, too young. I didn't fit in at school and soon gave up trying. I sought refuge with some childhood friends in Chingford. It was like being around happy people from stable homes or money was too hard for me. I was tremendously bitter and the feeling of being less than, inferiority and embarrassment from a child echoed through my persona as things were now worse than ever before; only this time, I had better choices.

I preferred to be around a different group of lads who had similar issues to me and just wanted to have fun, make money, and kick up dust, no politics or bullshit. It was all kids' stuff really, selling a bit of this and that, moving this and that, collecting and dropping off this and that for people. I flew under the radar easily as I was under the age of eighteen and about as white of a kid as you could imagine. I would wear ripped jeans and pink T-shirts and spike my hair to not only avoid the authorities but the set ups and traps along the way. People always know when things are coming and going and so why not allow the goods to be collected or dropped off, let them leave as if there are no issues and lure them into a false sense of safety, and then have someone rob them for everything they have? You get all the bits, cash, and none of the aggravation. There is no honour among thieves and these days it's brutal, friends killing friends on snapchat for 'respect'. I have never been a gangster or any kind of hardman, but I have always had a lot of friends in every one of these departments. I grew up with people who became notorious, I grew up with people who became Police

Detectives', and then I grew up to become who I became. Most of us came from broken homes looking for male role models in all the wrong places but ended up as our own little delinquent family with our own morals, values, and a shit ton of hatreds. It was our own little world, far away from the horror of our realities. Venting and supporting each other, in the good and the bad. Until one night we bit off more than we could chew, and my life changed forever.

One night in the summer some friends and I went to a house party in Chingford. The second we arrived you could cut the tension with a knife. We were younger but with a reputation for causing issues and being little shits; however, this was an older group's party, and we were the younger sisters' friends; the older sister friends just gave us pure shit from the second we arrived. My trouble buddy Danny... oh yes Danny! Let me introduce him with the respect he deserves before we go any further.

Danny was born into money, but he savagely hated it. Let me explain why. His father had always worked hard but when his mother suddenly died of Cancer and left him with two children, 12 and 8, he went into full fight mode and left the kids with his mother-in-law six or seven days a week and went to work. Building an industrial cleaning company from a good company into a monster in just seven years. Selling it on Danny's 16th birthday for over £3 million. This pissed Danny off on so many levels. He would hate me for saying so, but he needed his father not the money and had followed the same path as me and found great comfort in his rage. Plus, now he had money, and everyone saw him as a spoilt rich kid, which he made his mission to ridicule at every opportunity. Something he would re-educate you on if you were ever stupid enough to comment. He had everything but he was a shell of a boy who grew up filling his giant void with all the wrong things. A lost boy just like me. I would love to say we loved each other from the moment we met but our relationship is far funnier than that.

I met Danny in a way that pretty much defines our relationship until this day. I was dating a girl from Chingford and one night we went for dinner at a little Italian restaurant, two minutes from the police station. As we walk in all handsy and ready for a lovely evening, she noticed her friend who was also on a date, with Danny. They shrieked and embraced so excitedly I already knew what was coming. Danny and I were already clearly underwhelmed by the situation, weighing each other up and knowing we were now going to spend the evening on a play date instead of a date-date. Then it came, "oh shall we just sit with you guys? Double date!" Followed by more shrieks. I was fuming and thought Danny looked like a complete twat. Not looking me in the eye when we shook hands and trying to play the tough guy. Well, it turns out he was. It wasn't long before the girls went to the bathroom together leaving us sat there like two children on the naughty step. I couldn't take it anymore and ordered myself a shot and another beer, adding the same for Danny and telling him we might as well get fucked up, even in silence, as our planned evenings were clearly over. He laughed and we started talking more and more as the drinks flowed and flowed. After a while he asked if I wanted a line of coke, and we went to the toilets and did the business. But just as we were walking out of the cubicle and into the small hallway leading from the back of the restaurant through to the main dining area, Danny said something very silly. He made a joke about the girl I was seeing's ass. I stopped and he walked into the back of me. Nudging me forward and laughing, "what you fucking doing you nob?", he growled. I turned and headbutted him, splitting his left eye as he fell back into the wall. I casually turned around to walk back out to the restaurant. A terrible idea. He punched me in the back of the head and started bouncing around like he was possessed. I stumbled into the door leading back into the restaurant and turned to face him. It went off! We were windmilling and fighting so hard that I hadn't realised we had ended up in the restaurant and I was punching him over someone's back as they sat at their table. They were literally being forced into their dinner. The scuffle was herded out of the restaurant as panicked diners began attacking us for ruining their evening. But once outside, the door was locked, and I guess the police called because the police arrived in just a few minutes. They arrived to Danny and I panting on the floor in deadlock, trying to bite and gauge each other. Literally gripping each other and headbutting each other like a pair of lunatics as we lay in the street. I definitely won, just for the record, although Danny would disagree. To be honest, we both lost, and both looked ridiculous!

The police aren't like they are today, they kicked us, grabbed us, and cuffed us. As they should. When they stood Danny up, he dropped a genius line. "Bruv, what's mum gonna say?". I'll never forget it. Both coppers laughed and asked if we were brothers. I said that we were and had just had too much to drink. Again, the police are different now. Mostly geeks with a badge and it's all about hitting targets, but these two just started laughing and literally slapped us both around the head and gave us a huge lecture on how to behave before uncuffing us. We were told to stand with one of the officers whilst the other went inside. We both knew the game would be up as soon as any questions were asked so the second the restaurant door cracked open, we both sprinted off into the night. Danny almost stopped to go back for his jacket, priceless. But I grabbed him, and we shot across the road and into a small church yard before back-roading it up to Epping Forest before walking through the woods as I rolled a joint in the dark and Danny moaned about fucking up his shoes and his dam jacket. It's safe to say I never heard from the girl again, but I had made a "friend" for life.

Back to it.

As I was saying... Danny and I were standing in the garden smoking a joint with a girl Danny knew, and a girl I was dating (for context, she was black) when a guy in his 20s with an extremely spotty face walked over and started flirting with the girl. Danny laughed at him and looked at me saying "he wondered what happened to the milky bar

24

kid, sad bro, sad to see", all three of us started laughing. The Milky Bar kid then spat in Danny's face. Well, Danny being Danny, there was only one response. He knocked him out cold. Now, we were in trouble! The party erupted into the garden; people came pouring out of the adjoining kitchen and into the garden to get to us as we were already unwanted guests but ironically, now we were just wanted. We were fighting but I couldn't tell you who. People were jumping over others to punch us when suddenly this massive skin-headed monster of a man pushed through and pulled people off us like they were children, he was clearly in charge. As he did, we tried to retaliate but this big dude literally shoved us both back into the fence with one arm, "were you born stupid or did you take lessons, stay there you mugs".

When they saw we were kids it turned into handbags at dawn, a little shoving but it nearly calmed down to the point we could walk out of there. Nearly! Then a loud-mouthed cockney lad made a comment to the girl I was with about being with a white boy; she told him to fuck off but he responded with something stupid, "fuck off and take your Master with you". This time it was me who erupted. Bottles were smashed, faces bled, and Danny and I were pummelled against a fence until we literally fell through it, or it fell through. Who knows, I had a fist in my face at the time. We managed to scramble away before hurdling some fences and making our way out to the street. Scarpering like rats from a sinking ship as neighbours screamed at us and Sirens were getting louder by the minute.

We were in a bad way and with no girls around we were openly panicking as the guys at the party were not nice people and the girls were still inside. Suddenly the big skin head pulled up in a white Escort RS Turbo (the ultimate chavs car at the time, my dream car back then) and an even bigger black fella sat in the front seat, yelling at us to jump in. We were either stupid or fearless because we did. They told us the girls were ok because all the guys had left the house because he had made sure only girls stayed. Before I knew it I was pushed back into my chair as we accelerated down the road and around the corner, before the police arrived.

And that's how I met Jay...

Jay was a different beast. He was homeless at 14 and sofa surfed and slept rough until he was 16 when his uncle took him in. His uncle was as tough as nails. As tough as they come and standing 6 feet 6 inches, he was formidable in every way. Jay grew to an inch shorter and was genuinely one of the softest-spoken gentle giants you could meet. Only joking, he was a fucking beast who would actively seek bullies and anyone who wanted trouble, 24/7. He was an old-school gentleman but needed to vent or he would become like a volcano that needed to explode. The perfect example is a story his uncle told me, and Jay hated. When he was 15 a female friend of his was taken by two girls and two guys and essentially kidnapped to a house where they were doing terrible things to her like putting out cigarettes and not quite sexual but certainly humiliating acts that I won't mention out of respect to the victim I still know today. These were grown men and women, in their 20s. The girl's friend ran off and Jay happened to be nearby and they crossed paths. Jay knew who these men were and that the house was a drug den they used. Without hesitation he ran to the flat, unarmed, ran through the door, and beat up all seven men, and three women inside. He then threw two of the men off a second story balcony. Got his friend and carried her home a few miles away because she didn't want anyone to see her. At 15! The police were waiting with the terrified friend and her family I believe. That was Jay, the best of friends and worst of fucking nightmares. The police attempted to prosecute Jay can you believe that. Unfortunately, their selinenes resulted in more silliness and the two officers receiving phone calls that diminished their interest.

Safe to say my friendship with Jay instantly flatlined any issues I had with anyone because from the day I met him. He quickly became my big brother, the father figure I had so desperately searched for. Despite only being three years older than me.

––––––

Back home, we were really struggling and had hardly any food in the cupboards despite my mum working practically 24/7. Three jobs, seven days a week. Three growing lads will devastate the kitchen and I remember times my mum would cry as we raided the shopping bags as we brought them in, truly rough times and my heart goes out to anyone going through the same. Stick together and stick with it, the sun will shine again. My mother was like a god to me during these times. No matter what, she got up and started grinding every day to provide with a broken heart and bills coming out of her ears. Anyone who argues there's no such thing as an Alpha female mentality or that women can't do something, you're as ignorant as a Nazi, and I feel sorry for you, because I grew up with a front row seat watching proof of it day in day out.

So, at fifteen I was all set, no trust or belief in people, broke, wearing shit clothes and all round not a unhappy chappy. My family were hurting and watching my mum struggle every day created a monster. I would literally lead her to the bathroom mirror when she was at her lowest and telling me she couldn't go on, both of us crying. I would make her scream with me at the mirror, "Fuck them! No one cares. It's us, and we are a team, we don't need anyone." We were a fucking team, the best team ever. She was my hero, and soon I simply stopped worrying about me, I just worried about my mum, my brothers; and the fact that my mum just gave my fucking dog away because we couldn't afford to keep her. I don't know how to express this enough, but this was one of the saddest moments in my life and remains to be as I watched my mum heartbreakingly give our dog away and return home to us kids who wouldn't even speak to her. However, Bella pissed all over the persons house and they brought her back. We were all so happy but that feeling of not being able to afford our dog truly changed me.

A couple of days later my mum's uncle Dennis came to the house, arriving in his Bentley. My mum asked him to borrow money and he said no. I was upstairs at the time but listening intently and at this point I came downstairs. My mum had led him into our tiny kitchen desperately showing him we had no food but Dennis simply said, "I don't do those sort of things Sally". I nearly attacked him there and then. My mum pleaded and said that he was her mother's brother and she needed help. I couldn't take it anymore and told him to leave whilst he could. One side of my family live in stately homes and have true wealth, unfortunately my mother's mother died when she was four years old and her father, my grandad was a terrible person by most accounts and so the family stepped away from him and his four children, my mum being one of them.

I realised here that it was time I stepped up fully. It was time for me to start making money and all that meant was saying yes instead of no, easy as that.

I spoke to Jay and he offered me money, but I didn't want charity and he didn't want me involved in drugs. So, one night before school I was at the Moon Under Water pub in Enfield with some friends when an older lad we knew walked over to me and offered me some items on tick (no money up front, I could pay him after I sold them). I told him I would meet him where he asked in an hour and ran to get my Ford Orion. Yes, I was only 15 but we all had cars back then as the driver's license was a paper copy, no picture. I met him in an alley not far away and when he showed me what the items were, I had no idea what I was looking at so called a girlfriend of mine and she came down to look. I told her to play down whatever it was but to flick me and tell me not to waste her time in future if they were good and I should buy them. The second the door to the van opened she flicked me to within an inch of my life. I bought the lot and my girlfriend and I went around selling them in pubs, hairdressers and even held an open sale at her mother's house the next morning. I sold the lot in a week and filled the fridge and cupboards at home with a glee in my eye and swollen heart. Pride, it had been a while. I told my mum one of my friends gave me the money. I think in this situation my mum chose not to ask any questions. She was happy for the relief. I then began hiding money in her bags and coats, just little notes so she could keep her pride. She was paying the bills all alone and no matter how hard she worked we couldn't keep up. Soon enough we had to move out of that beautiful house into a far smaller house where an old man had just died. The carpet was funky green, and the passages were too low for us to walk through so had to duck or hit your head, like I did on the daily. This was when I lost a bit of niceness, bitter that we always had less than those around us. I had a huge chip on my shoulder. I started boxing but left the gym after fighting with some of the guys outside the gym. I was the only white lad and they treated me as such. A family friend then got a grip of me and started training me. Coaching me in the real alpha mindset and how to act correct on the streets. A real face, Alan 'Oli' Oliver.

Oli was a real player. He had a very hard upbringing and was respected in the top circles of criminality. I won't say anymore on him or his activities as in this case it wouldn't be right. Just know he was a legit face and someone that quickly became a great role model for me at the time. Slapping me into shape and teaching me how to act on the streets as well as in the gym. At this point he treated me at my mother's son but soon things changed.

I was at David Lloyd's gym in Enfield one day working out with a couple of friends of mine discussing last night's mostly fabricated conquests, when Oli walked over and asked me for a word. Truth be told he wasn't asking what he was telling, and he knew that I knew that because he was not only a friend of the family but also legitimate face not around London. He had heard through the Grapevine that my friends and I had been involved with something and the people knew who we were and had reached out to him to manage this gently because we were young and I was a linked to him; but these guys were serious guys who wanted their bits back and were more than prepared to hurt kids who decided to act like adults. We were lucky for Oli in this situation, even if my mates couldn't see it.

Oli told me there was someone I needed to speak to and walked me straight from the gym into the David Lloyd's car park and into the back of a Range Rover parked on Donkey Lane, where he jumped in the front passenger side. I in the back. In the driver's seat sat a rotund Irish man who, before he spoke, didn't look intimidating whatsoever. Oli politely introduced us, and the Irishman shook my hand and said it was a pleasure to meet me. I was shitting my pants at this point as I realised the guy had Oli's ultimate respect which meant he was a very serious person and if I had upset him in any way, I would be in trouble it would be very difficult to get myself out of. So, I kept my mouth firmly shut and ears open. But all he said to me was exactly that; it was lucky it was me and we have a mutual friend (Oli), he would "call the wolves off" but they wanted their bits back immediately; to which I told him no problem and I apologised. We shook hands and I looked to Oli for permission to get out of the car. I walked all the way back through to my friends in the gym before giving them the great news as straight as I received it. They all complained until I offered them the opportunity to go out front and tell them themselves. We had to take the L, but some losses are worth the lessons – if not the contacts you make and air you get to keep in your lunges.

Oli then took me under his wing, which meant he kept me in check by telling me he would batter me if I fucked up again, so I got more shit together and was quieter about my activities. This kept me out of trouble despite him laughing as he bollocked me, he got a buzz from it, sharing his stories of when he was young. He was a very good boxer and taught me how to fight. He had a brutally hard life but made something of himself and broke free of all the bad things to find a bit of peace. He saw me making all of the wrong moves and started teaching me boxing and the harsh reality of being a man. He would spend hours talking to me about the psychology of men, of love and war, the possibilities, and pitfalls of life. He would preach to me about being mentally strong enough to control my emotions and channel them in the right areas of my life. He was the first to show me that discipline is freeing, not constricting. How discipline can achieve anything, and I wouldn't need to fight or conduct criminal activities just to get by if I just focused. Naturally, it fell on slightly deaf ears, and I took it all with a graine of salt at the age of 16, but as I grew older, and especially as I matured, joining the Royal Marines and throughout my life, this resonated with me and ever word proved right beyond measure. I now realise what he was trying to tell me all those years ago. He was trying to tell me the juice has to be worth the squeeze in life, and you need to do everything for love, not through hate or for reputation because you will only scare away those you need most and attract those with hate in their heart, just lie the hate you put out into the world, you get back. You will have money and respect, but you will know how you got it and it will never be worth what you did to get it.

Training with Oli and having a male role model who knew the score was priceless. One day when I arrived at his house early for training and long before having a mobile telephone; he wasn't home so I went to use a phone box close to his home and while sitting on my bike calling him, two lads came up and put a knife to me punch me in the face took my bike and we're gone before I could really think let alone do something stupid like get myself cut. After walking home massively pissed off, I found Oli at my house with my mum, both concerned as I had been lost between the two. I told them what happened, and Oli said not to worry, and we would go and train and then he would buy me a new bike. Instead, we left the house and once away from my mother we drove around local estates where he threatened everyone he could find until I got my bike back.

He then bought me a new bike lock and bits as he felt guilty, he didn't have to, but I was over the moon as this bike was better. After that, every time I went through those estates, I was left well alone. Now many people will judge you for seeking the warmth of a Dragons wing but I would often suggest that you do not understand the history of the dragon who is often simply damaged from their suffering in life and this is the circle in which we must break and something that I learnt very young in life as I had so many friends that suffered far more than I, and I knew how hard I found life.

Oli grew up in institutions and spent time in prison but had an absolute heart of gold. He knew how hard our situation was at home and went out and bought my mum a car. However, all good things come to an end. One day I was at an ex-girlfriend's house when my mum called me hysterical. Yelling that Oli was going crazy, and on the way to collect the car from her. She was scared and this was crazy to me so I rushed home still not understanding why Oli would act this way; he had always taught me to respect women and he loved my mum. So, for him to be talking to her this way I knew something must have happened. I lost my mind down the phone and told my mum don't worry if he wants a war, we will give him fucking war. It was important she knew I was there to protect her even though I was shitting my pants. But I meant it. I drove home and made her a cup of tea, tooled up whilst chatting to mum, and waited. However, I had completely overestimated the situation and he just messaged me to say something like, I know it's your mother boy but don't get involved, put the key in the ignition and I'll drop someone off to collect the car. He came, took the car, and I never spoke to him again. It later transpired my mother had gossiped about him and caused him a lot of problems, I stayed aligned with my mum, obviously. However, it was only a short time after this that Oli was stabbed to death while walking his dogs in Enfield. The dogs had got into a fight and Oli ended up getting the better of the younger man, obviously. But the coward waited and ambushed him from behind, stabbing him in the back. Just like that he was gone. I just went out and got high with my friends. Not even mentioning it until a couple months later when it was in the newspaper and the lads asked. Life goes on and so do the lessons we teach others. I learnt a lot from Oli, the main thing was the importance of focussing on self and maintaining accountability for ourselves at all times, no questions or days off.

RIP mate.

Chapter 2

GROWING UP WITH ANGELS WITH DEMONS

D espite aspiring to be a real problem on the streets, I was a dedicated and dutiful son at home. After taking a year out of education, I did as my mother asked and attended Hertford Regional College to study Media, Production, and Communication; I wanted to become a TV presenter. However, looking for attention or even suggesting such a thing whilst mixing with the streets, even to the low level I was, is never something that ends well; especially when you looked like a Backstreet Boy. I always found myself fighting to prove myself, maybe more than most, maybe it just felt that way, who knows? My head was a tornado at the best of times back then. Especially once I joined college to improve myself, as anything considered self-improvement or elevation will always be deemed an insult to those who choose to cement their roots in the position or situation you are trying to escape, as bettering yourself reflects their own lack of ability or energy to do so. This is why your biggest supporter is someone you have never met, and your biggest hater is always someone close to you. I felt like I was always fighting growing up.

I was never a gangster or tough guy; I am not trying to paint you that picture at all. I just didn't give a fuck and the pain I felt inside meant all external noise was toned down whenever I would fight. It's important you grasp this as there are so many plastic gangsters and wannabes out there and I was never one of those, nor did I hang out with those idiots. I was either with good boys, or very bad boys. My two personas. I always felt the odd one out no matter what group I was in, and my anxiety would sometimes literally make me go blind, my vision fuzzing mid-conversation with someone. I would die before telling you that back then. I had become a master of keeping my friends and "lives" separate. Often telling friends I was with a girl when I was with other friends and even had different phone numbers for different people and groups.

Being the rascal I was, I would use college as a cover and arrive early, register, and then duck out via the rear carpark because it wasn't covered by CCTV. My friends would collect me so we could handle business that needed handling with the perfect alibi. Collecting Danny in a similar way which distanced us from each other as well as from what we were about to do. The much older guys who picked us up and set things up would always stay well out of the way whilst we did the business, before acting as our getaway drivers. We used them to handle little issues for us too, like robbing drug dealers we couldn't, or getting information, but we were well aware that we were disposable so Danny and I always had our own backup plan. Sometimes it would be something simple like delivering something from A to B, then C. Even if we got caught back then we wouldn't be violated like kids violate each other today, not as casually anyway. You had to have done something or have something significant to get shot or stabbed.

The drivers would often wait out of sight, but close by in case things got naughty. However, most of the time we were robbing the people who gave us the information in the first place. It was regularly a single mum who was the baby momma of someone involved, paid to keep money or drugs in their house. If not, we would simply knock on the door with a clipboard in hand, and they would open as we looked like a couple of innocent white boys... we would put our foot in the door and explain we were coming in one way or another and they would hand over everything they had. Or, on other occasions we would literally run through the door, wait for them to return home when high on their own supply, etc, and then smash through the place within minutes before getting out of there.

The best scenario was inside information from the baby mommas. It was actually civilised. We would hide a chunk of the cash hidden at a place of their choosing for them to collect later, and would often kick in the front door and mess the place up as we left to protect their involvement. We found it funny because we wouldn't tell them what we were about to do. They would then call the poor old dealers / baby daddies and tell them it was a couple of black lads instead of two Backstreet boy wankers, as instructed. This worked the other way round too. It worked so well, why wouldn't we use it over and over again. We would get our black mates to do the same thing, although it would always be an older person driving a family car. Not us in my Orion.

Things were not always smooth and looking back I must have been insane to get in the mix of all this. Because if I was caught it would not have ended well for me, but adding stress to my mother and brothers was my main concern, I legitimately didn't give a fuck about myself back then. I just wanted to fight and fuck away my pain. And when that didn't work, I drank and smoked until I couldn't anymore. Selfish really, but at this time in my life I chased anything that would make me feel, just feel; I was numb to everything and only felt alive when losing control. This became a casual activity for a while, but these things always catch up to you.

One day Danny and I knocked on a door to conduct the usual, but the guy was in the house. Before we could speak, he had flown out the door and started smashing us all over the place, ending up in the stairwell. Danny and I were swinging for the fences but were getting our asses handed to us big time when he tripped over, it gave us an opening. He stumbled down the stairs and we were trapped above him. It was something like the 5th or 6th floor on a cheeky estate and we had attracted a lot of attention. I remember laughing nervously as he stood back up, then I kicked him square in the face, but this jacked coke head was running on evil, and he brushed it off like it was nothing. Jumping up and smashing me against the wall. I remember feeling no pain but instantly sick as my world flickered. Then I heard a thunderous crack, and the barrage stopped. I looked up and saw the most beautiful sight. Our drivers had heard the commotion, like every other fucker within a mile of us. They could have left without reprisal, but they were as good as their word and came running to save us. Literally. My head was spinning all over the place and the ringing in my ears was deafening as the boys dragged me stumbling down the stairs and shoved me in the back of the car. We accelerated down the street and Danny jumped into the driver's seat, swapping with our mate to avoid the police (black faces are pulled over far more than Bieber faces) and the three of us hid in the footwells of the car until we were back in Epping Forrest. We changed cars and clothes, as per usual. A very close call, I have the scars to prove it.

Danny called Jay and told him what had happened, he went berserk! He had no idea what we had been doing and despite the ringing in my ears I could hear the venom in his voice and knew big bro wasn't exactly going to turn up and kiss me better. As predicted, he turned up and Danny had to run into the woods to get away from him. I was sick whilst holding onto a tree and as he walked past, he kicked my arm away, so I lost grip and fell forward onto my face. I just laid there for a second before rolling over to an absolutely raging 6ft 5inch meathead telling me everything I already knew. Long story short, we had fucked up and it was going to come back on us. Jay knew the responsibility would be his in the long run and that wouldn't have bothered him but the fact we went behind his back enraged him. The lads we tried to rob didn't mess around and Jay was worried for us and let us know in his own special way. He was just disappointed, either way, he would be with us to the end.

I finally managed to get into Jay's car without him pulling away each time I got anywhere close. He was finally calming down and laughing at the state of me. Not the situation, not at all. But at the state of us and how lucky we had been. After hearing him go on for an eternity, I eventually told him to "shut the fuck up and skin up". He burst into laughter and said, "OH! morning sweetie, how's your head you little bitch?" He slapped my head playfully. Telling Danny to wrap a joint, who passed it to me to light. However, as I started to smoke things went foggy, I was sick on myself and then unceremoniously passed out. The concussion was real.

I woke up being dragged out of the car but quickly found my feet. I was all over the place but jumped into Jays Escort RS car; well, I fell in, and we shot off down the road at warp speed. When we got to Jays we got rid of our clothes and showered. Danny helped me because I couldn't lift my arms. He took great joy in punching me in the nuts for fun but claiming it was to test my responses. I sat on Jay's bed for a couple seconds before he walked in grumpily, gave me some clothes, slapped me lovingly and told me to "fuck off home, your bro's will be home from school soon...".

I was cooking dinner for my brothers that night when I felt something wet running down my cheek. It was blood, coming from my left ear. I fed my brothers and went to bed feeling very sorry for myself. My head was pounding, as if Big Ben was chiming in my head. I couldn't sleep and laid there worrying about what would happen next. I had bitten off more than I could chew this time, it certainly wouldn't be the last, and I certainly wasn't alone. At this point in my life, I was so used to conflict and being held accountable for my every word and action, that I had become addicted to it. The honour and loyalty I found among my fellow delinquents didn't exist with normal people in their normal lives as they scurried around shitting on each other to get ahead in the rat race. I simply could not understand living my life that way, as I know they could not understand my choices or lifestyle. Anything but a normal life and having to accept the cards I was delt. I would rather burn the casino down and watch from a hillside with my friends as we flipped the world on its head. The world didn't want us... no problem, we had each other.

Things at home had begun to settle a little as my other life went berserk, the balance of life never fails. I had the sense to lay low and started spending a lot of my time with my college and Enfield friends. Adam remains my brother from another until this day, his family welcoming me as their own. We spent most of our time smoking weed and chasing girls. But I couldn't shake the constant simmering anger, a direct contrast to Adam, who remains one of the most placid and removed humans you could ever hope to meet. Not me though, I still needed to vent. I would regularly drive to Chingford to hang out with Jay, Danny, Ryan, Leon, and Wez despite knowing I could hide away in Enfield without drama or concern. No one knew my real name or where I lived. Besides, I had a "fuck it and fuck them" attitude at this time because the only place I ever felt safe was with my wonderful angels with demons; our individual traumas and self-destructive behaviours melting away whenever together. We had a brotherhood that we would purposely put to the test at every opportunity, because we all needed the constant reassurance that those around us would be there no matter what. Fearlessness and raging insecurities have and always will be a deadly cocktail of fuckery, but the cure is often more painful than the disease and those who need the most love are often the hardest to love. I was and have always unfortunately been one of these lost souls, despite my fingers burning as I write this. But it is true and also a reason I am as tolerant as anyone you will ever meet.

Oh! How rude of me... apologies I got lost in the story. Allow me to properly introduce Ryan, Leon, and Wez. Ryan was a big ginger traveller descendant, Leon a little black cockney wide-boy with more energy than a Duracell bunny on Cocaine, and Wez was a very quiet and funny mountain of a man who could intimidate you simply by being in his presence. He was only around 5 foot 10, but he was roided to the max and could bench 200kgs when he was 17 years old. Funniest thing was, Leon and Wez were cousins. (FYI, these were not their real names).

These were seriously chaotic times and I always felt like people were watching and judging me as my insecurities convinced me the world could see my pain. As if I wore it across my face like a big ugly scar. I would often go to my room and scream into pillows or blare my music so loud my mum and brothers couldn't hear. Things had become more complicated as my father introduced his new girlfriend to us, destabilising my homelife further as my mother become overwhelmed after almost finding a rhythm, but hid it from my brothers with such class and grace it blew me away. At nineteen years his junior, and only ten years older than me, this hit my mother hard and caused her to act out in desperation to find her own replacement. Despite working six or seven days a week and being a genuine hero to my brothers and I, she needed more, she needed a companion. She set an example each and every day, showing us what it meant to take accountability, and what it meant to have a genuine alpha mindset, even when all the odds are stacked against you. I cannot explain in words how much this version of my mother inspired me to become the man I am today, as I developed an anything is possible attitude and became obsessed with taking extreme ownership as I witnessed the results first hand. Although I hadn't quite learnt how to accept the things I couldn't change, in fact I still struggle with this until this day, accountability was instilled in my fabric and it has served my pursuit of excellence ever since. The forever unreasonable man.

My mum rarely ate at home, so we could. Never complaining in front of my brothers, instead retiring to my loft converted room where she would cry, and I would console. Then when she stopped and went back to reality, I would cry my eyes out at seeing my hero so hurt. I would then go out and look for a fight to make me feel better. It wasn't rocket science, but it worked. Physical pain cannot compare to emotional pain, in my opinion. So a cut here and there was always a fair trade.

My father had introduced his new girlfriend like fuel to a fire, but what else was he to do? I knew he had been with her prior to the breakup, as did my mother, but my mum would never admit it to me as she knew I would have likely burnt their house down just to show her I had her back. I had caused enough chaos in my own selfish venting and feared it would overspill into my home life soon, so decided to retract to an emotional support for my mum. To this day I have never had an issue with my father's now wife or their beautiful kids who I adore as if my own, but it is in these brutal times that I recognised my father's ability to dodge any form of accountability like Neo dodging bullets in the Matrix. So, anyone who thinks alpha mindsets are inherently male, you are more wrong than you could ever know. Again, this is how I felt at the time and only mention it so you understand my headspace and my journey. My father is a nice, loving, family man these days and today we have a relationship I cherish. But back then it was wonky at best.

A dutiful son and brother by day, venting lunatic by night. It was so mental it worked. Stabilising my mentality enough to function. A toxic balance of duty, denial, and ignored feelings. Some days I would be hoovering whilst making deals, attempting to use the hoover to mask my conversations from my ever-listening little brothers. What a muppet mindset that was.

My brain was a hive of anxiety and fury as I questioned my every thought and became increasingly frustrated as my simmering temper worked as a defence mechanism to hide my pain and crippling fear. My only release was losing my shit and projecting my bullshit into the world and towards anyone who even suggested they might challenge me. I soon became more comfortable in a fight, than in a cuddle.

I remember my mother always wanting to cuddle me for her own comfort but at this stage in my life, I just couldn't. I could barely look her in the eye. Her touch and eye contact were enough to break my machismo exterior, crumbling me into her little boy again; someone I simply couldn't afford to be anymore, even if I dreamt of it. I left my baby brother to this who would jump off the sofa and out of mums embrace at the very sound of the front door unlocking. Seriously cute, but I struggled to even witness this as I rejected any form of comfort and love as I forced myself to become the man of the house. Forcing myself to harden up daily. In my mind anyway. I rejected comfort and sought discomfort. A single crack in my armour might cause hesitation in the streets and that would be a far higher price for my mum to pay than a missed cuddle. I was genuinely fearless, if not borderline psychotic at the time as I felt I had nothing to lose and everything to gain; I hated myself. Desperate to prove my worth to friends, girls, perceived enemies, and anyone else who entered my atmosphere. Loud and obtuse, as if to bait people into testing me, I was a pure prick at times; worse, I was proud of it.

Fearful people are the most dangerous people when they don't take accountability and channel their fear into positives; instead, they become overwhelmed into irrational behaviours and erratic reactions. Forever poised in survival mode, searching for triggers to justify their fear and irrationality. Whether this is to act violently, or worse, toxically. Their irrational thinking and unpredictability a threat to everyone around them, especially themselves. Their commitment to this position must remain in place or they risk losing the comfort created by their delusionary comfort zone. To recognise their tactical manipulations and subjectivity would be to undo their perception of self and create cause for change; and change is scary at the best of times, let alone to someone already waste deep in rituals, habits and reflections devised to avoid accountability at all costs. Trust me, I was the personification of the person I am describing back then, and my unpredictability scared me. I couldn't make sense of it... because it made no sense. Creating a painful cycle of anger and frustration I spat at the world as if I were the righteous one in all of this. When in fact I was my very own worse enemy. Justifying my actions by demonising others instead of recognising my instigations.

In my opinion, manipulation and toxic character assassinations are far more dangerous than violence. I am in no way condoning violence – I have seen more than most and advise anyone to avoid it if they can. I mean that from the bottom of my heart as it took a lot of violence for me to become this gentle. However, in a one-on-one situation there is an opportunity for that person to defend themselves, or at very least a choice to walk or run away from the conflict all together. However, in a toxic attack situation in which someone weaponizes lies and rhetoric to gain vantage or destroy someone without genuine reason or notification, many other people are involved and hurt in the process. It is a coward's sword, and destroys more lives and damages our community more than any drug ever could. Simply to reinforce a single person's narcissism. Just look at cancel culture. Lies reinforced by lies to create separatism. I learnt the art of these tactics later in life when I worked for agencies who excelled in the execution of such tactics. The huge difference being, back then I was learning from my own experiences and seeing how violence was almost pure in comparison. The lesser of two evils in comparison to the problems disseat instigated. For example, have you ever had someone judge you for your reaction to their disrespectful actions? They initiated the issue and then attacked you for your response to it, acting as if you were the initiator of the conflict. That is the definition of manipulation, and some have it down to an art. A tool that serves everyone from spouses to the people who run the world, and everyone in-between. The degree massively varies but it is very much a part of human nature and one we must all be aware of if we are to avoid such pitfalls.

Well, what has this all got to do with anything... please allow me to explain my discombobulated reader.

I have witnessed this tactic cause catastrophic and lethal situations in my life, resulting in my friends killing my friends and people going to prison for life. All because a weak person chose to be a catalyst for violence instead of accepting accountability. Often for nothing more than attention. This is why I am so obsessed with accountability. It is the key to knowing your true self and the subsequent loyalty, humility and honesty that come from it.

Empowering those who recognise it to utilise their intuition and perceptions to avoid or protect themselves from situations those lacking either create or sleepwalk into. I have seen so many avoidable violent situations become tragic due to such miscommunication or misinterpretations. Fear removing the option for peace, and when someone with a fearful narcissistic mentality is central to such a situation, it becomes intensified at their pleasure as the capability to communicate is removed through their framing to avoid the truth presenting itself, exposing their motives and instigations.

Growing up this was perceived by all those I respected as the worst kind of human. And one night I saw first-hand just how extreme things can get when people refuse the truth for "their truth".

Hanging around with my not-so-little crew of misfits removed this level of bullshit and held me to a standard of accountability long before the Royal Marines would: Jay, Danny, Ryan, Leon, and Wez made me feel a part of something. We showed each other love and support that I had never experienced before. I was never involved with gangs and certainly never even close to being a gangster, but both were always around and planned or at least inspired a lot of the naughty situations I got into. I learnt very quickly that so-called savages are often more civilised than the so called civilized because they understand the repercussions. Freedom and safety aren't free. Without the supposed safety net of the authorities, we were forced to take accountability for not only our words, actions, and environment, but the words, actions, and environments of our friends and associations.

I was taught this lesson one night after an earlier seemingly nothing interaction turned into a huge something. We were all sitting in Jays car waiting on someone who was late, meaning we were in a place we didn't want to be for longer than we had to. Whilst waiting I jumped out of the car to go to a shop around the corner to grab drinks and rizla for the boys. When I walked in there were two girls in the shop arguing with the owner about some nonsense. They were being extremely loud and abusive. I ignored the drama and B-lined for the Haribo and drinks. After getting what we wanted, I walked to the counter to pay and as I got to the counter that was next to the exit, two lads I half-knew walked in and we said "hi", literally "hi". I waited as the girls continued to gob-off at the shop worker. The two lads finished getting their items and as they approached the counter, I asked the shopkeeper if I could pay. In all honesty, I did so to avoid the lads I knew doing it first and making me look like a bitch, possibly even causing issue between us. But without missing a beat one of the girls turned to me and shouted, "Rude! Wait your fucking turn white boy". I said nothing, I knew the area I was in, and this was normal. However, the guys I knew were now stood behind me and had no such issue. One snapping, "Who da fuck ya think ya talking to ya sket?", the other following up, "Move yourself. Chatting bare shit over nothing, leave da man alone". The lads stepped in front of me and before it got physical, I threw money on the counter and walked out.

I walked around the corner as three lads walked the other way, nearly walking into me and doing their best to do so: one kissing his teeth in the process. I hated that shit! But ignored it as we were there for business. I got back to the car and the lads gave me shit for taking so long. By then the guy had come and gone, so we could go. As Wez jumped out to let me get into the back seat, the three boys and two girls came bouncing around the corner, losing their shit, shouting all kinds of racist threatening shit at me. One of the guys was screaming something about a "honkey hitting up his sister". This wasn't good. We were parked in a dead-end and as I mentioned this wasn't a friendly area for us.

It wasn't his sister; it was just an excuse to regain face after they got into it with the two guys I knew in the shop and got a slap in front of the girls, no doubt for gobbing off to my friends. The age-old mantra, chat shit, get banged as valid then as it is today in London. I could care less as I sat eating Tangtastic Haribo in the back of the car, but Jay and Wez felt different. Jay told me to jump in the driver's seat as he got out. I ignored him and got straight out of the car as Ryan did the same. Danny jumped into the driver's seat and started the car. Jay and Wez were already out of the car and trying to talk to the guys. But once brave, the guys became nervous when they saw the size of Jay and Wez. The girls escalating their verbals until one of the guys pulled a gun. It was the first time I had seen one. I couldn't believe it and couldn't believe Jay and Wez were unfazed as they continued walking towards them, intensifying their verbal and body language with every step. I was shitting it.

The girl started pointing at me saying I had hit her and one of the guys was saying my mate from the shop had stabbed him. Turns out he had. He had certainly been stabbed but he certainly wasn't my mate, and I was long gone before they even arrived. The girl wouldn't shut the fuck up and was screaming and screaming until people started coming out of the woodwork. Throwing shit off overlooking balconies. Flowerpots, cans, bottles, all kinds of shit was smashing around us.

It turned out these girls had tried to steal from the store and been caught, choosing to then go on the attack and be racist towards the Indian shop keeper's wife. The husband then came out to defend his wife and that's when I entered. The perfect storm.

The gun had stagnated the violence but the verbal arguing intensified. Then the guys I knew from the shop came bouncing around the corner and mayhem broke out. The guy with the gun turned to face them and as his did Jay and Wez ran at them. I was hit from behind and stumbled into Danny. A group of men and boys had flooded out of a stairwell unnoticed by us. We just put our backs together and produced some world class windmilling. Taking and giving blows without aim or consideration.

Jay and Wez were now fighting across the road from us when the gun went off. No one was hit but it was an incredibly rare thing to see and hear gunshots in London back then, so everyone scattered. Danny jumped in the driver's seat again. Ryan and I dove in the back, Wez jumping across us; Jay jumping in the front passenger seat of the already moving car. Danny literally drove through people to get us out of there as the gunman made his way towards us. Something he had to do to get us away but it would come back to haunt us.

As we drove down the road Danny realised he had been stabbed in the leg and was bleeding badly. He pulled over and jumped in the back so Jay could drive. It was quite bad, and blood was all over my legs as I tried to elevate the wound in such a small space. I had no idea what I was doing. We had to get him help and fast. We got to the hospital, but Jay wouldn't drive into the hospital grounds because he didn't want his car associated with the mess we were in. A seasoned and smart move but at the time I was going berserk! Danny was conscious but bleeding, groaning, and screeching vengeful, tear-soaked threats. I was arguing with Jay until he got out and dragged me with him, smashing me against the car, telling me Danny needed help and I needed to get a fucking grip. I got it together; we got Danny out of the car and Ryan helped me as the three of us hobbled into the hospital grounds. As we entered A&E I expected help to come running from every direction, but this was far from reality. Security attended before any medical support which only intensified the situation; three teens covered in blood and clearly distressed, and security is first to arrive, I went nuts. However, when they saw Danny was in a bad way the security guard saw sense and shouted for a nurse. Helping the male nurse put him in a wheelchair before he was whisked away to get the help he needed. I was asked to sit down in the waiting room after saying I had no injuries, and the tubby security guard calmed down and went back to eating his cake at reception.

I had been sliced across the back of my neck but hadn't realised at the time because my adrenaline was pumping. So sat there in a packed A&E waiting room of sick, angry, and miserable people, I began feeling sick. Ryan had kicked off with security so left to calm things down after I told him I would stay with Danny. Then the adrenaline dump came hard, and my vision began to blur. I was looking at the ground when the same nurse came around the corner and told me Danny was going to be ok but was going to be kept in. Oh, and the police had tried to ask him questions and would be out to speak to me shortly. That was my cue to exit. I stood up and the room spun. I gripped myself and walked to the bathroom, I took off my hoodie, turned it inside out and soaked it in the sink. Washed myself with it whilst fully clothed to remove as much of the blood as I could, then causally walked out of the hospital. There was far too much going on for security to notice me leaving. I called Jay and met him back at the bus stop he had dropped us at. He pulled up like a F1 car pulling into the pit-stop. As he did, I saw Ryan wasn't in the car but another guy we hung out with from time to time was. Let's call him Harry. I jumped in the back with Harry, and we shot off down the street. I could tell tonight wasn't over yet.

Jay told me that Harry had been told by people on the estate what we had been involved in and that one of the girls was the sister of someone we really didn't want any issues with. However, Danny had been stabbed because of this bitch, so now it was whatever it had to be to make things right. I was fucked already, but it seemed we had become pretty good at this fuckery malarky, so it really was nothing new. I hadn't been paying attention to where we were going as I listened to Harry talking us through our best approach to the situation, when

we pulled up outside Ryan's house. He came out, arguing with his mum, as he did on the daily. He passed me a bag through the window and went back into his house before coming back out. Arm around his mum. He kissed her and told her not to worry, and we were off. We passed around sharp or heavy bits and bobs as we set off back to the estate.

As we neared the estate, no one had spoken a word. We parked a few streets away, and before we got out Wez said something along the Shakespearian line of. "This is for Danny boys, and they called it on not us, so let's take names and brains and bounce out quick; we need to get in and out fast and fucking hurt these cunts and hurt them bad or they'll be back. Harry knows the way so follow him and when we get there I'll lead, Harry will lead us back". I was clearly shitting it. Only 17 and tiny compared to the others. But I nodded along with a screwed-up face that had seen better days. Wez looked at me and lovingly slapped my face, laughing and saying "my n*****, you got this brother! For Danny yeah".

I was shaking as I got out of the car; my adrenaline surging for what felt like the 1000th time that day. But I had never done anything like this, and the cocktail of fear and fury was making me shake uncontrollably. Wez and Jay cut intimidating figures at the best of times but when they were together and in this mood, not to mention armed, they were terrifyingly, even to those who were with them. This boosted my confidence as I began to hype myself up thinking about Danny.

We cut through the labyrinth of alleyways, Ryan behind me breathing heavy and speaking softly to himself, he was ready! We came out of the alley opposite a small playground where the lads we were looking for always hung out. Surrounded by four-story flats, and everyone they knew, or at least knew them. There was no point trying to creep up on them so after a silent nod from Wez, we burst out of the alley and hoped the 3ft fence around the playground, steaming into them before they knew what was happening. Surprise and ferocity were our only option, and it worked a treat. I wanted the guy who had got Danny, but in a situation like that there's no order, this was pure violence and violence is chaos. But if I got the opportunity, I would make sure he knew it was me who got him. We were animals as we steamed into them. I smashed one man across the chest with a bat, sending him backwards onto his ass, and causing me to drop the bat. Ducking as it fell to grab it but I was kicked which caused me to spin, landing on all fours, not a place to be in a fight. I grabbed the bat and jumped up, I lost my shit and the mist descended as I lashed out like a berserker, smashing everyone I could, as hard as I could. Within seconds the group were spread across the ground like butter. I turned and began stomping and smashing the ankles and shins of the fucker who had stabbed Danny. My fear turning to rage and burning away all my humanity as the thought of losing my friend drove me to smash and smash and smash until someone grabbed me and a familiar voice shouted, "Let's go, they're done!" It was glorious mayhem that lasted maybe a minute if that. I couldn't tell you. If you told me 30 minutes, I couldn't argue. I heard someone shout from the alleyway we came from but couldn't make out what they said, the mist still clearing. Jay pushed me in the direction of the alley and I fell over an unconscious body as I turned. We ran back to the car in what felt like seconds. Ditching our tools over fences and in gardens as we ran. Harry was driving as my heart stopped pounding enough for me to hear anything other than my pounding chest.

We dropped Wez and Ryan at their place. No words exchanged. Jay and I went to his. We had won the battle but were now in a war, and in war there are only ever losers. Winning is never worth the loss required to win. And the juice must always be worth the squeeze.

Chapter 3

WE ALL GO THROUGH THIS LIFE ALONE, TOGETHER

Jay had become more than a big brother from another mother and put an end to all the little hostilities I had brought upon myself whilst trying to make money. Jay had replaced Oli for me in my endless search for a male role model despite only being four years older than me. He had become the idol and example I was subconsciously yet so desperately searching for; fearlessness personified, and a how to guide to quell my constant feeling of impending doom. Always putting others before himself even when it meant his life would be threatened. There are so many things I cannot say in this book as it affects other people, and I would never ever do such a thing. Not to a celebrity, friend or even enemy; but Jay and I were thick as thieves, and we had each other's back and proved it to each other time and time again.

One day three guys went into a pub we used to frequent. They were looking for me and had been very loud about it, beating a few people up to set the tone and smashing random patron's drinks from their tables. When they left, a girl we knew called Jay to say who had done what. It was totally uncalled for and caused over the fact a guy had gone through his girlfriend's phone and found messages between us. He then called me with his friends in the car to regain respect as the altercation had happened in front of them. I answered and when I heard his voice not hers, I was instantly worried he had put hands on her so went from zero to 100. He asked me where I was and started threatening me so I very maturely told him I was in bed with his mum, but she was almost done, and I would be back over to see his misses shortly, so would meet him there. He stopped talking at that point which meant I knew he was serious; how could he not be, I had removed my enemy's opportunity to retreat. I asked if he was still there whilst laughing provocatively. He said coldly "Where are you bruv?". I told him, "Don't worry, I will find you". He hung up. I knew this would be an issue, but he had multiple girls on the go, and this was about pride not love, so I wasn't too worried. Anyway, he really took it to heart and started calling people linked to us both to find me. Someone eventually telling him I might be here or there, so here and there is where he went until the aforementioned situation occurred.

At the time, I wasn't aware Jay had been called and was now also calling around. Eventually finding out they were in a small gym he knew the owners of. Basically, a drug dealer hangout. He drove straight there alone, parked outside, leaving his car running, apparently not through planning, but rage. He walked through the door and up to the three lads to ask if they'd seen me (mocking them) and without breaking step steamed into them. Annihilating all three of them in seconds, before picking the main guy up and putting him in the boot of his car. Driving him to Epping Forrest, stripping him and then putting me on the phone to him so he could apologise.

I know many of you will be reading this feeling sorry for this guy, and it may seem overly brutal, but I loved him for this. After all, this is the world we had all chosen to be in. Besides, that piece of shit ended up raping a 17-year-old girl later in life and died in prison of an overdose. So, he was no saint.

I had always felt alone in the world, feeling the world was against me, but here was someone willing to protect me to this level without me even knowing. Not exactly what you would call a mainstream hero but it's funny how one man's freedom fighter is another man's terrorist, and when the shit truly hits the fan, and most of you will hopefully never know that feeling; I promise you, you would feel the same. Those guys would have hurt me badly and Jay knew it. He was acting out of love and every true soldier fights because they love what is behind them, not because they hate what is in front of them.

To have that sort of love and protection is one of the greatest things I have ever experienced. Impossible to replace and is the definition of loyalty where I am from. Throwing yourself on a grenade not meant for you, so to speak. Many will claim with manicured words that they will always be there for you, have your back, are your ride or die. But most are fickle, fearful people, hoping their words inspire your loyalty and service, not to offer theirs.

Convincing themselves that they have acted, but without action, commitment, or consequence. The tightest circles are united through joint suffering, overcoming or against mutual adversity: Character and loyalty are not built-in ivory towers, and in the spoilt western world we now all live in, I fear my generation is the last to know such deluded selflessness. I pray I am wrong.

Jay was the first person I ever spoke to about joining the Royal Marines, and he thought it was an awesome idea and would have joined with me if he hadn't a criminal record. Genuinely, he wasn't one of "those guys", all of us Bootnecks have met who claim they almost joined, did join but a comet hit the train on their way to sign up or some other blah blah bullshit. He came with me the first time I went to speak to them at 17, but I wasn't able to join as I had a little legal issue or two at the time. It was later expunged, a story for later. Anyway, I left with my bad attitude still intact and thinking the Royal Marines were crazy to turn me away. I am sat here laughing as I write this. Imagine the delusion of that kid who saw it as his right to join such an elite unite of legends. Raw belief, fuelled by fear and fear of becoming a normal person had led me to delusion. It didn't make sense to me, but the Corps instils discipline and creates virtuous savages, it doesn't teach little shits to become big shits to cause mayhem. That is what prison is for. I wish I had been able to join back then as it would have done me the world of good, but in all honesty, I think I would have acted up and ruined the opportunity in one way or another. I wouldn't have quit, but would have been acting a fool in and out of training as I just hadn't matured yet.

Life went on regardless, until one night my life flipped upside down and things were never the same. I was laying on my bed watching films and hanging out with my girlfriend. Jay called and asked me to come down to a club he was working at that evening. We laughed and joked for a few minutes, but I ended up not going to the club, choosing to stay at home with my girlfriend. Obviously, you don't go to McDonalds when you have a steak at home. We hung up after lovingly abusing each other, saying that we will catch up tomorrow. That was the last time I ever spoke to him.

I'm not sure how long my phone had been vibrating but it was long enough to wake me up from a stoned stupor. It was my Danny, he was hysterical. I could barely understand him but heard "Jay's in hospital"; I was dressed and out the door within seconds. I stayed on the phone to Danny, and he began to calm down enough, so his words began to make sense. Tearing into me as they did. He told me I needed to get down there as soon as possible, saying, "he might not make it brother". I laughed, "Of course he will brother, its Jay".

I got down there and parked, and the lads came out to meet me so we could talk. It was retaliation for the shop-inspired gun incident. The tit for tat continued. The mist descended and I don't remember getting out of my car, I don't remember walking through the hospital corridors; but I do remember seeing Jay's mum's face as I walked through the door into his room. That face haunts me to

this day. I saw my friend laying there and went into shock...
the room spun, and I went numb. How could this happen?
HOW THE FUCK COULD THIS HAPPEN!!! I exploded
into a volcanic rage that no words I write here today will
do justice to. I exploded verbally and physically and had to
be restrained. Can you imagine being his mum or pregnant
girlfriend as I threw this selfish temper tantrum, no matter
how I felt. I'm ashamed to this day. But I was just a terrified
kid.

All they were going through and now I was screaming
the hospital down, projecting my fear and pain for all to
hear, like I was special. I was only a kid but that was selfish
of me. In that moment I was ready to rein in hell even if I
had to destroy heaven to do it. Such rage will hurt who you
love most, and I was about to truly learn this lesson. Danny
came bursting through the door pursued by a nurse trying
to pull him back. I pushed the nurse back through the door
and stepped outside with Danny, grabbing him tight as we
crashed against the wall in a flood of raging tears. Wez
appearing and dragging us around the corner to a waiting
area as he calmed us down. Checking us. "Oi, that's his
fucking mum and girl in there. Man the fuck up boys. We
got shit to deal with. Save it!". Looking back, he was so stoic
it was scary. Not me, I was all fury and brimstone, an
emotional wreck. I felt terrified and at fault, if only I had
been there! He was always there for me, and I had let him
down. I couldn't believe this big strong hero of mine was
laying with tubes coming out of him, so vulnerable. A
doctor came out of the room and told us that he wouldn't
make a full recovery, his brain had suffered too much

damage and been without oxygen for too long. Jay's mum and girlfriend just fell to bits. I don't really remember how I felt or anything but the next thing I remember is following Wez and Ryan showing up.

We walked towards the hospital exit when Wez started losing his shit, setting everybody else off too. We got into it with site security and then argued with the police who wanted us off site. As we were getting kicked off the hospital grounds, Jay's mum appeared and begged hospital security and staff to let me stay as I was "family" but agreed everyone else would go and she would be sure of it; the lads felt hurt by this as we were all family and took out their frustrations further on the hospital security. Ryan eventually getting arrested. But all the emotional and physical tension was instantly mitigated by Jay's girlfriend. She appeared and screamed a scream so full of pain I can hear it now.... "STOP IT!!!". Everyone stopped in their tracks. The boys turned to leave as the security turned back to their duties, the magnitude of the situation outweighing all procedures and egos. They left and I stayed at the hospital that night, in that horrid small waiting room of pending doom where others are getting bad news throughout the night, the type you pray you never hear.

I didn't sleep at all. In the morning I took Jay's mum a coffee as she slept on a chair next to Jay, a machine breathing for him. The doctor came in and said we had to leave for a few hours. We finished our coffee and said goodbye to our boy. I then took his mum home so she could shower and rest a little. Planning to collect her and Jays girlfriend later that morning. I then drove to Jay's house to take care of some things for him. I was still there when Wez called me and said he would take the ladies back to the hospital so I could do what I was doing, and he'd meet me at the hospital when I was done. Around 30 mins later I was all sorted and showered. As I got into my car Wez called me to say Jay had passed away. They had arrived a few moments before. At least he wasn't alone.

No words were said between us, Wez had just said "he's gone bruv"; and like that... life was never the same. I hung up from Wez without either of us saying another word, Jays mum was calling. I answered and she was stoic! The strength in her voice as she asked me if I wanted to go and say goodbye to my friend is something I remember well. As if this was the last thing she could do for her boy, and she would do it with class. I couldn't go. I began punching my steering wheel and going berserk until the tears came and kept on coming. I crawled into the back seat to hide from the world and cried and cried until my chest hurt and my eyes burnt. I loved that man, and he loved me. Losing my first ever true friend cut me deep, almost in two if I'm honest. I nearly lost the nice part of me that day. All kindness and softness holding on by a string of humanity. I felt alone and just wanted to be. I climbed back into the front seat of my car and drove to my mother's house. I can't remember the drive and didn't remember it then either. It was now early afternoon and I found myself sat on my mother's sofa, wishing the world would swallow me. How could this have happened? I already knew exactly who had done it. But I wasn't angry yet. I was in disbelief. Lost to the world.

Sat on the sofa trying to compose myself, my mum inconveniently came home from work. My poor mother came home from work for lunch and found me in a state. We had a heart to heart as we hadn't really spoken in a long time and had become like ships passing in the night. I told her as much as I could tell her, she had chosen the wise decision to never ask too many questions a long time ago, so I did my best to hide it all. She was suddenly thrust into my reality and hadn't seen me vulnerable in the longest time. But that was over now. We had a big talk. I already knew what had to happen next and she was worried. She tried talking me into eating something and sleeping but that sounded insane to me. I told her I would be ok but wanted to see my friends. She never knew any of my friends as I kept everything out of the house, but she understood.

Love, trust, and loyalty is the holy trinity of any relationship and in my eyes, Jay was watching me, and it was my turn to step up, the pain, even humility of not going to the club that night to be with him was burning holes in my head as I drove to Danny's house. I was dangerous in this moment, zero morals as the thought of revenge conquered my being. I would have burned the world to the ground in that moment if I could. I was numb to everything other than hurting the people that dared to step into my hell thinking they reined. Tonight, I would rein and would happily suffer any consequences.

I arrived and Danny opened the door before I knocked, Wez and Ryan were sat in the kitchen. The conversation was much like you can imagine. Ryan was hysterical, Wez silent but good to go, Danny just cried. We knew exactly who had done it and who had helped them. Then the call we had been waiting for came. A car was set up for us with what we wanted, none of us talking as we got ready and walked the ten minutes separately to the prepared car. Wez putting the phone on the loudspeaker so we could all hear. Wez said one word "driving". We shut up and watched Wez get us through the traffic as the car following our prey kept us updated on their movements. Trying to beat them to a specific road (choke point), we drove slowly to not draw attention. However, they cut left instead of a right, taking them off course to where we thought they were going and our friends were unable to follow or they'd be exposed.

The car was silent as we pulled up at the traffic lights in Walthamstow. Suddenly Danny spotted the car on the right-hand side of the large cross junction.

Now it's important to say at this time we didn't realise exactly who was in the car, but we recognised the car and the driver. Whilst the boys were arguing about what we were going to do, I just got out of the car. A chorus of "Where the fuck are you going", and "What the fuck are you doing" following me.

I have seen the CCTV footage many times, but it is like watching a movie for me, I do not really remember it; I jogged across the intersection, almost casually, the guys saw me coming. How could they not? They started to get out of the car. Then I started running at them and threw my bat at the windscreen as I pulled out another weapon. Two of them then ran at me and we start scrapping. I genuinely don't remember any of this. The red mist blurring the lines and primal instinct taking over. I was a lot smaller than them, but my ferocity was overwhelming them. They were likely stoned and having a lovely day when this crazy little Backstreet Boy looking bastard turned up in full demon mode. I destroyed two of them and by now Wez had driven through the lights and had pulled up in front of their car so they couldn't drive away, their driver had attempted to drive off as the two lads jumped out but stalled, which in hindsight suggested they had things in the car they couldn't afford to get caught with. Now things were about to get really bad for them. Wez had driven through the red light and across the intersection section and drove into their car so they couldn't go anywhere. I don't even remember hearing the crash and the car nearly hit me. The boys jumped out and joined the fight, all hell breaking loose. Another group of them suddenly arrived from nowhere and the fight swung in their favour as I was knocked to the ground.

I was on the floor getting smashed but didn't feel a thing. Rage! It was these mother fuckers who killed Jay, the big bro I never had. I was possessed with hatred. I was suddenly able to come to my feet as the boys smashed and cut at them. I have a moment of clarity where I remember smiling at one of them as I stood up, I wanted to eat their souls in that moment and hoped I died with them so I could hunt them in hell. I was lost to my pain and the guy's face dropped as he saw this possessed fucker would have to be killed to be stopped. One of them began to run away as the police sirens drew closer and I started to come round as I was further enraged as I wanted them to be monsters,

I wanted to see the eyes of evil who took my friend from me but instead all I saw were cowardly humans. How could humans have done such a thing! I exploded again, I wanted all the smoke, I wanted to burn the world twice over and let the universe see this is what happens when you take a friend of ours. I was screaming nonsense at this time and joined Danny in his fight as mine had left the party.

I picked up a kosh and hobbled over to help Danny who was getting beaten against a car like a rag doll. I realised this was the guy who opened the fire exit to let them in. The guy who set Jay up. The fury raged again, the hatred overcoming every niceness in me as this mother fucker dared to breath as my friend lay dead. This was THE guy. I would have killed him and died happy in that moment. I smashed him across the face and blood shot across the car. He fell. Danny and I stamped and stamped, screaming at him. Danny bent down, biting his face as I kicked and kicked. This was beyond rage. Wez had been stabbed and I couldn't see Ryan. Suddenly, I was flying. I was thrown around six feet in the air, into a car, winded and broken, I got straight back up but fell again, my body shutting down. I couldn't stand up and kept falling all over as I was attacked by God knows who.

This had all taken place in minutes. A single police car arrived and then van after van, and they weren't messing around. They steamed in and started smashing us all to the ground. Not one of my friends or I tried to run and kept on fighting until the police had us in cuffs. They all tried to run.

70

Wez was sat next to the other guys at first as his skin tone matched there's. But he leant over and headbutted one of them. Climbing on top of him whilst cuffed was mounted headbutting him in cuffs as two police tried to stop him; before a third arrived and knocked him out with a baton across the head. Danny, Ryan, and I were left laying on our sides behind a van in the centre of the cross-roads. Wez came round and started screaming, asking where we were. We were shouting back. I could barely talk at this point. The adrenaline dump hitting me hard and my rage turning to tears as revenge had come and gone and my friend still wasn't with me.

A policeman walked Wez around to us to calm the situation, but Danny was recognised by a female police officer, and she was physically shocked. She knew him and how old he was. The police pulled us all up onto our asses. She came over to talk to Danny but at this point we were both losing our shit again. I tried to get up so a copper picked me up and put me in the back of one of the cars, Danny was thrust through the door after me. We were checking each other's injuries whilst crying in rage. The female copper got into the front of the car, calming us down saying they had found guns and drugs in their cars, and they would be going away for a long time. She smiled but we didn't care.

The reason the car had tried to drive off is because they had a gun in the car and the reason the other group turned up is because they had drugs in their car. The gun car was the look out. They had just re-upped. Silly bastards should have got the drugs out of there, but these weren't geniuses. Lunatics and scum bags mostly.

I realised in this moment I wasn't a gangster and didn't want to be. Losing a loved one in this way can never be righted. Revenge is short lived as it's never enough. Ambulances arrived but we wouldn't let them near us. The police then drove us to the station and once the vehicle lock was secure, they let us out to smoke cigarettes and gave us a hot drink so long as we allowed the paramedics to check us out, which they did. Shock setting in. I was shaking and weeping like the boy I was. A scared boy. I was taken to hospital, as were the rest of us.

Ryan was in a separate hospital and Wez went straight into surgery. Nearly dying from his injuries.

Danny's dad came down to visit us after getting a call from the police and I refused to give my details, so they were stuck for what to do with me. When Dannys dad arrived he told the police my name and that I was his nephew. The police could not have been nicer and as we were kids and they had seen the footage they simply could not understand what had caused us to attack such formidable people.

Danny's dad Brian left after a few hours, but I was asleep long before that. Only waking up as Danny shook me awake, saying we had to go. I was wearing overalls they gave me as they kept my original clothes for evidence. Danny had been given spare clothes by his dad and being the legend he was, Brian had taken Danny clothes and told him to get out as soon as he could, and he would be waiting to drive us home. So, there I am all fucked up and Danny turns up with a wheelchair saying to the police we just wanted some air. They let us go and we got collected and spent a day or two recovering at an undisclosed location in Essex. Everyone we knew heard what had happened and began supporting us in what would obviously not be the end of the street issues, let alone the start of our legal battle.

A couple of days later I went around the back of my mum's house to break in as I had lost my keys. It was Wednesday late afternoon by now, but no one was home. I had a shower and smoked a big joint and went to bed. I woke up around 3:00 AM in the morning and drove to Jays house. I just wanted to be near him.

Chapter 4

SALTY WOUNDS

I woke up to the sound of someone trying to break in. I crept into the room and saw someone I knew squeezing through the bathroom window they'd just popped out. Obviously there to steal the stuff I had moved from the house when I came back from the hospital.

I waited until he managed to get his second shoulder through the window and as he looked up, I grabbed him; pulling hard and smashing him onto the bath floor. I fell back in pain as my body was still battered from the days before. He stood up and we started scrapping and scrambling, moving from the bathroom doorway into the front room. As he pushed me back onto the sofa, one of his mates kicked the front door through and joined him in punching me. I was pretty banged up from the fight the previous day and got a bit of a kick in here too. I squirmed my way off the sofa under a lot of weak punches and flipped the footstall over to grab the Rambo knife tapped to the bottom of it. It wasn't there, fuck! I found an opening and ran to the bedroom, managing to get the knife hidden above the bedroom doorway, now we were even, two against two. I chased them out of the house and down a street or two before running back to the house. Coughing up blood and feeling like death now that the adrenaline had worn off. There was blood everywhere, most of it mine but from wounds earned before these muppets tried their luck. I didn't feel a thing as I fixed the door and called a female friend of mine who lived down the street. She came right over and knew everything that had gone on so was more concerned about me being out of hospital, let alone running the streets armed to the teeth, chasing future crack heads. We cleaned the place, well she did whilst I laid on the floor moaning. She insisted I go to her house where she wanted me to stay until I was healthy, maybe even eat and sleep properly, it had been a while. I agreed.

I had planned to sleep then go look for the guys the next day but as we were leaving the house my friend asked who had done it. I told her it didn't matter, and she shouldn't ask me things like that, but she persisted and said she might know where to find them. So, I told her. She literally stopped in her tracks and turned to face me. She told me she had been to a small party not far away, hence just getting home when I called her. She told me the guy I mentioned was at that party and left the party proclaiming he was going to get "a load of party snacks" for everyone. She looked me in my eye and said, "come on I'll take you to his yard".

I called Danny to let him know what was going on. We drove to the person's house. I got out of the car and ran straight through the front door. I ran up the stairs and beat the shit out of this guy in his bedroom, whilst fending off his girlfriend. Danny arrived and ran straight into the house, guided by my female friend. I threw him down the stairs to Danny, we stripped him and left him in the street, leaving promptly as we honked our horn so all the neighbours would see what a pathetic little man he was. Apparently, he was a friend of Jay. But I guess not.

There were no comebacks or issues over this and I would have welcomed them anyway. My soul was on fire, and I craved anything to stop my head from melting into itself with the reality Jay was gone. The self-destruct button had been firmly pressed and anyone who wanted an issue was more than welcome to it. This is truly the most dangerous human being I have ever been. The ferocity, the fear, it resulted in absolute zero fucks being given about anything or anyone, and the bitterness coursing through my veins made me nasty and void or moral values. I wanted to see the world burn. The way I saw it, the world wanted a monster, no fucking problem, my fucking pleasure. I would give it the most monstrous monster they ever did see.

My female friend went home, and I jumped in the car with Danny. She was begging me to stay with her as she knew that's what I needed to get better. A few days in bed being cared for, fed, watered, and dare I say, loved. Instead, Danny and I went on a couple week bender where we even got cautioned by police for fighting each other at one point. We were causing mayhem; robbing everyone we didn't like; we were completely out of control and getting into it with some seriously dangerous people. Eventually the inevitable happened.

One day we were drinking in a pub that backs onto a golf course when three guys approached us and picked a fight, we should have seen it coming. We stepped into the rear car park and were snatched into the back of a van that sped off as we got slapped into reality in the back of it. They drove us a couple hundred meters at speed before pulling into a small muddy car park. The van doors stayed shut and the guys beat us until we stopped talking shit, and then added a few more beats until I was barely conscious. Then one of them said - "First AND last warning cunts!" - we recognised the voice, and we stayed silent. Turns out it had been an opportunistic thing as they had just come to the pub for a drink when they spotted us and took advantage, a fair one. Play silly games, win silly prizes. To this day I don't know what we did to him, but it must have been something because he was old school and to snatch us like that we must have really taken the piss. However, I still do not know exactly. Say no to drugs kids...

Completely and utterly by coincidence of course; The following day I received a call from Jimmy who I met through Oli, a well-known man involved with everything and everyone. He told me I should go and see him asap. I went after a cheeky McDonalds and joint, grabbing Danny on route to share my pain. Jimmy hated him so I always got an easier time if he was there. We walked into his pub and Jimmy came straight over and went absolutely berserk! People began leaving the pub whilst Danny and I stood rooted, trying not to laugh. Jimmy walked off and as he did Danny whispered to me, "Thanks' for the fucking invite mate", and we both laughed. Jimmy turned around and slapped Danny square across his mouth before grabbing me by my throat and growling, "Oli would be ashamed of you boy". He meant it, his eyes burning with fury. "Embarrassed of me?", I said almost laughing. I was still drunk and should have known better. Danny definitely didn't, he laughed again, "that's worse than angry mate, fuuuuck!" Jimmy told him to get the fuck out, but Danny went to talk instead. Jimmy dropped him. And grabbed me by the face this time. Danny sat up. Jimmy let go of me and sat down at a nearby table before politely ordering three pints of Guinness, I hated Guinness from the barmaid who hadn't battered an eyelash over our little telling off.

We sat down gingerly. Jimmy then gave me some of the best advice I have ever had. He told us he wasn't mad but needed to make a point. The point being, if an old man like him could slap us about, we had to imagine who else is out there and what they'd do to two little cocky lads like us? He told me there was money on the street to find me and that I had to go away for a bit. I refused as I had my mum and brothers to worry about, but he didn't want to hear it. However, within a month or so I was in Sydney, Australia with my mum in the most awesome hideaway ever. A beautiful home in Manly, Seaforth, Sydney. With a whole new world to explore. Away from all the madness.

However, first we had court. Wez and Ryan had been tried separately the week before as they were classified as adults. Wez had priors and received six years but ended up doing nearly nineteen in the end after getting into some trouble inside and whilst on release at some point or another. Ryan got two and a half years, so it would be fair to say that Danny and I were justified in shitting ourselves over the fact that we would likely get something similar. However, on the day our lawyer told us a transcript and CCTV materials and statements had not been presented to the court in the designated time and therefore would not be considered. This was apparently amazing news for us. It was. We walked free that day and straight to the pub where we proceeded to get shit faced. Jimmy called me and kind of congratulated me but followed up by saying I still had to go away so he could smooth over things for me. So, I did what any reasonable man would do, and went on one last bender with Danny before leaving with my mother for Australia.

My mum needed a break and had been struggling with my brothers who had grown into a huge pain in the ass for her at the best of times, so they had been spending alternate weeks at my dad's house. My brother James was always an asshole, and she couldn't manage him and needed a break. And I knew repercussions didn't just go one way and that the money was already out for information, so this worked perfectly. We were so excited to be going away and Australia was so far away from our realities, it really was perfect timing for us both. We laughed and were still so close at this point, it felt like it was us against the world. I was able to be a son and she was able to be my mother for the first time in years, as everything else dropped away and we could just be us.

I was far from perfect, and perfectly fine with that, but I needed to refine myself if I was going to assimilate with society and be a success at anything positive in life. I had hidden myself from the world as I hid myself from myself, in an attempt to achieve what I needed to achieve, without my feelings getting in the way.

Leaving London and seeing my mum show glimpses of her old self was wonderful. I was so proud of her and had a front row seat to her struggle but with enough grace and strength to hide it from my brothers. Until this day I hold other women to this standard of accountability and value. Even her! I am blessed to have met many wonderful and inspiring females in my life but my mother at this time remains the most impressive person I have ever met, my hero. Broken inside but her exterior like iron. It makes my heart swell with pride at our little team back then.

We were on the plane and my mum opened up to me. She told me she was worried about me and wanted me to promise her I would consider going to University. She didn't really mother me anymore and had begun to see me as her support structure first, son second. And having this conversation was difficult because I felt I had gone too far to go back to University. Back to studying? How? I needed a challenge, but University sounded like a bad idea. I wanted to spread my wings and make Jay proud of me, but university? In proffered the sound of the Royal Marines. Besides, how could I tell her everything that had happened and expect her to still look at me and see her little boy? She knew there was trouble but not the severity and that's how it stayed. Until she reads this book like the rest of you.

Honestly, from the moment we boarded the plane we were like mother and son again. I took full opportunity of the free noodle's alcohol treats and films whilst she slept the entire journey, clearly needing the rest. We were collected from the airport by her friend in a convertible and taken to the incredible home of her friend we would be staying with.

Australia was an oasis away from the nightmare that was London. We adventured and travelled around Sydney together. It was amazing to watch my mum blossom day by day out there, but I knew she would be going home without me soon; she had made me promise to stay away for at least six months. I was worried those who promised to protect her wouldn't stick to their word or be focussed enough but I genuinely enjoyed watching my mum soak in the good life she so deserved and realised I could make that happen for her back home if I got my shit together. I remember praying she would find a kind, successful man who could look after her. She deserved it after everything she had been through.

We had been struggling and her Australian friend was living an absolute dream. It was a sign things could be better. It inspired me so much, to step outside of what had become such a small world of negativity and struggle with no example of what we were struggling for or what life could really be. We would laugh and say one day we will have all of this... We went on lots of little adventures, always talking and laughing, but the elephant in the room remained; my mother was always pressing for more info, more questions about what had happened.

Her time came to an end, and we had a very tearful goodbye at the airport. I enjoyed being my mother's son again and being away from all the drama, I knew things had and would change but it all started with me.

I nearly had a panic attack as my mum was leaving as I would be unable to protect her from the other side of the world. Although I was trusting her safety in people who I would call to protect me, the feeling was terrible as I was scared something could happen to her whilst I was so far away. My mother pulled me to one side, hugged me tightly, kissed me and winked at me before telling me to man the fuck up, jokingly. She told me that she would be absolutely fine but made me promise her two things before she walked through security; Firstly, I had to promise to have fun and "be silly" for a while. Second, when I finally returned to England I had to go to university or find a career path and something on the straight and narrow that would focus my energy positively and allow me to heal. I knew she was right and a huge part of that she said meant removing myself from my group of friends, I had to change everything. I was so emotional at the time I agreed to everything, she walked on water to me, so why wouldn't I.

After my mum left, I tried to be nice to myself like she said, but found myself having a ferocious inner dialogue as I battled with my demons; I focussed on trying to pull the positive thoughts to the forefront of my mind for longer periods each day but the negatives were always there to overwhelm me if I didn't pay attention. The internal dialogue would sometimes over-flow and I would speak out loud, embarrassing myself. I preferred being alone anyway. I was out one day partying and by the time the bars filled at night I was drunk and had made some new friends.

Making friends with a group of legendary Irish lads who were travelling the East coast; The next morning I had booked a place on their coach tour, departing the following day. I still hadn't been home the morning we were set to travel. I literally ran in, grabbed my stuff, and bounced down the road in the back of a pickup with my new friends on our way to the coach station.

I was about to experience Schoolies in all its glory. I couldn't believe it when I saw it. If you haven't heard of it, google it immediately and you will understand what an epic a party this is. Held in the perfect location on the Gold Coast, it turned out to be just what the doctor ordered. I met people from all over the world and partied for ten days straight. I let loose and found myself being more like the old me. I was enjoying myself, dancing, chasing girls, and just being silly like my mum had ordered me to. It was amazing and exactly what I needed.

People weren't ignoring the fact I was slightly removed or distant here, they would openly mock it, as did my awesome Irish crew. Girls jokingly mocking me, playfully teasing me out of my own head and into the party, cutting through my walls to lighten me up and be my unhindered self. It was just the medicine I needed. Girls from London are famously cold but the girls in Ozzy were forthcoming and confident and dragged me to the dancefloor before I could even answer. I was on the dancefloor feeling awkward when one of the girls came up and kissed me. I realised she pushed something into my mouth with her tongue and accepted it willingly. Knowing it would only make the day better. It was ecstasy and after she gave it to me, she disappeared into the crowed, coming back 20 minutes later with a beer for each of us and a joint to puff-puff pass. She got me to follow her, and we sat on this small hill side next to the dancefloor and smoked, before we had finished, I could feel an incredible rush up my spine. It felt great. Nothing made sense but nothing mattered. The girl kissed me again and we were off to the dancefloor. I felt amazing as ecstasy filled my body and I danced and danced; surrounded by thousands of young people all partying and having the time of their lives, I felt alive again. Dancing and watching the beauty that had led me here dance as the sun shone brightly and the DJ dropped tune after tune, to the delight of the crowd. My attitude was accepted back home but here my intensity and volatility embarrassed me daily, but in this moment, it was gone. I didn't feel bad for having fun as my altered mental state allowed me to be free. I thought of Jay, but thought how much he would love it, how I wish he was there but felt like he was with me anyway.

Let me tell you, that dance floor was my church and it helped me more than any religion or therapist could have at the time. I will never advise people to take drugs, but in this moment, I could see the light. I felt free as I danced my troubles out of the forefront of my mind where they had been sat for so long. I realised I could feel different and that my history wouldn't necessarily be my destiny unless I chose it to be. But in that moment, nothing mattered, and I could let it all go, nothing but me and the bassline mattered. What a moment.

Later that night, laying in a hammock with my new friend, I had this feeling of levity and literally felt a weight physically lift from my chest, causing me to gasp. My friend didn't even look at me and just said; "That's it baby, let it all go". A moment so profound I still think about it now. No one had ever spoken to me so casually about something so deep. Like a time of perfect synergy that caused a single tear to run down my cheek... the relief too beautiful to hold in.

That was it, I realised in that moment that I needed to get busy living and make something of my life, or I would be consumed by my demons and end up just like Jay. It was a harsh reality but as I let go of the construct of me. This bad ass little fucker who wasn't scared of anyone; I realised I was terrified or at least uncomfortable with every aspect of my life. Over time I began realising that all my bullshit was insignificant to my bigger picture and recognised a genuine opportunity for a different life, one I never knew existed before, or at least didn't want to pay it the attention it required. I just let myself go and stopped talking to anyone other than my close friends back home. In one night of partying, I realised just how much I had lost myself and was flying through my young life trying to be anything that kept me and mine safe. Ferocity is a great deterrent, but my word is it exhausting.

It's funny how a little bit of love, attention, and being thousands of miles from anyone you know can help you gain perspective. I was finally becoming aware and willing to at least begin getting over my own bullshit. I had been holding onto bitterness that I saw as memory or holding a candle for Jay. It did nothing but hold me back from becoming the person he wanted me to be. By holding onto my anger, I felt I was holding onto his memory. But here I could speak openly as it would not descend into anger or victimhood. Sat here with people from all over the world, our conversations were without conflict and open to ideas on things like gratitude, and how accountability and tolerance are key to self-empowerment. Endless conversations on the link between mind, body, and soul. My friends back home and I would talk about fighting, fucking and money, only. Here I was exposed to a different version of myself. I realised how my choices and decisions had manifested my current situation. I had chosen to hang around the rough places with the bad boys and had gotten exactly what many often get when walking this path. I was angry and disappointed but happy at the same time as despite this recollection being extremely humbling, I found hope in it as this meant that my life was a result of my choices, and I could change those choices to keep a very important promise I made to the big bro I never had.

Throughout the rest of my trip, I seemed to merge this new mantra with my ever-snowballing obsessive ambition to elevate my family and I out of our survival mode existence, and into a life of affluence in the sun. I had to change everything, or nothing would change. I knew if I put all my energy into the positive steps, they would lead me to the life I wanted. I knew I could do it, even then. I just had no idea how hard it would be.

Travelling Australia turned out to be the best thing I could possibly have done for myself. I saw the bigger picture, and now I was going home I was set on painting and framing my own future. I had become tolerant and subsequently open to the other, but I worried I would revert to my old self once home in the ends with my friends. I knew the biggest battle would be me vs me, but at the same time I knew just how stubborn and angry I was. Everyone else thought they knew, but they had no idea.

I went back to Sydney and enjoyed a relatively quiet few months. Spending most of it alone and thinking a lot. I wanted to get my mind right and get used to my new mindset before I got back home to all the bad things. I landed back in the UK armed with my new positive mindset and ready to make shit happen. I was my own boss and about to take extreme ownership to change my life; then Jimmy called. Summoning me for a "catch up". Being my own boss would have to wait a little longer. I made my excuses to my mum and went to his pub where I found him ceremoniously sat in front of the fire with a drink. He had one for me too, so I knew I was in for a speech; the old dog loved to set a scene before a speech. There really is something about old-school London gangsters that insist on a show. I was right, but what Jimmy would say would resonate with me so deeply I can almost remember it word for word, paraphrasing anyway.

"A lot of people have been through a lot of trouble for you boy and I am not going to let you embarrass them, you hear me." Well, he wasn't exactly Shakespeare, and what he actually meant was... he has put his name to me and protected me and if I disrespect that, he will be worse than those he's protected me from.

I went home that night and started my new life the very next morning...

––––––

I spent the next couple of years redefining myself and generally trying to keep my head down. Boring, but good. I used to tell myself. I had to learn discipline in every area of my life. I learnt that discipline is doing something you hate to do, but doing it like you love it. Without discipline you will give up at the first opportunity or available excuse, but discipline is freeing, not constrictive. It would take me a while to learn the latter as I fought the system at university after attending as my mum asked. I kept to myself religiously but found a lot of people had very little life experience and spoke stubbornly of newly learnt theories they would regurgitate as if they spawned the idea. They all had very little life experience and they annoyed me beyond words. I hated them. Not because they were bad people, but I realise now I was angry at their ignorance's, their belief in the system; I was insanely jealous they were so sheltered as I felt like a rusty shed at the end of their manicured garden.

I had a girlfriend I adored at the time, and we spent all our time together. Even working together. She was wild but would have had to be. We would work the VIP boxes and I became a restaurant manager at Chelsea Football Club, promptly positioning her as my head waitress. We had a great time, and I embraced this new life and relationship that helped smooth my transition immensely. We made good money and would have sex all around the stadium and at exclusive events we were running. Good times and a great girl, we are still in contact today. But University wasn't for me and despite getting my degree, I was ready to catch a flight out of the UK. I had known Journalism wasn't for me when I interviewed Ken Livingston. He was nice enough, but I had been sent down as the sacrificial work experience muppet from a local newspaper to not get an interview. The editor thought it would be a waste of resources to send someone else all the way to South London. So, I went. I turned up high as a kite and just started drinking and gorging myself on the buffet. He came over and asked me what was good to eat. I told him everything, I was high, of course it was. We got chatting and he asked what my job was. I took off my name tag and told him I was a student on work experience. He then asked if I would like to ask a question. I did, I got the quote on whatever bullshit he was lying about that day and went back to the office. The editor's first response was to call me a liar. He then confirmed the quote was genuine with a reference code I had been given by Kens staff, aligned with my name and publication. The editor was amazed. I quit that day. He was so excited about something so pointless I knew it wasn't for me.

My degree in Journalism, News Media, and Cultural Studies was finally cast aside for good after going through a long recruitment process and getting a job with over 1500 original applicants; only to turn up on the Monday with my suitcase. I was on the way to Spain, not a life of silent desperation living others dreams. I politely told them I was very thankful for the opportunity but there was someone else who would kill for the opportunity and therefore deserved it more. They respected me turning up to speak to them in person and I left on good terms.

I went straight to the airport and to Valencia, Spain to see my friends. I needed to get away and felt I had repaid my promise to my mum. By now she had a long-term boyfriend who kept her company, so I decided to go and do me. I was so excited to be leaving the UK. I arrived in Valencia and nearly died within minutes of entering my new apartment as Adam decided to jump on my back and nearly sent us both over the rail of the terrace. This set the tone and the next year was pure carnage. We started the festivities with an epic three-day bender. Sushi, Champagne, cocaine and an introduction to Latinas and their awesome culture that I adore until this day. Family, mañana-mañana, and baby... baby... baby.... It was genuinely one of the best times of my life.

I spent the next year or so having the time of my life. It was so much fun just letting lose and living the simple life, no drama. I got to be a kid again and renewed the fact that spending time with your true friends is the best possible way to spend your life. In the presence of your people, and amongst your tribe is always a good place to be. It was so much fun but after a while I had the partying out of my system and it was time to make something of myself. I had vented enough and was ready for the next stage in my life. My brother from another mother making the final decision for me.

I had been talking about joining the Royal Marines for years. One day I was moaning about being bored, Adam told me to stop winging and to go and join the Marines or shut the fuck up about it. We had a little play fight, and I went to get us lunch. When I got back Adam told me he had booked me a flight home the following Monday and I should go and talk to the recruitment office. I was genuinely blown away and could see he was sad that I was going but the fact he would help me make the leap is something I will never forget. You're my boy Blue!

I flew to London for a meeting with the Royal Marine recruitment team. At first it was a nightmare as I had a degree, and they were insistent I join as an officer. I wanted to be one of the lads so refused. After some negotiating and essentially waiting for the officer to leave one night, I managed to get signed off for my medical and aptitude test. The aptitude test was simple but the medical was one of a kind. A weird female medic getting me to do naked push ups and squats. Clearly, she was a weirdo, but she passed me, so I didn't care. Much.

I received my date for the Pre-Joining Fitness Test Plus (PJFT) and went back to Spain for yet another, yet final wild weekend, before flying back to the UK to abstain, detox, and train every hour god sent to be ready for the most arduous military training on earth.

Chapter 5

BECOMING A BOOTNECK

I landed back in London and got to work. I had been extremely dedicated to partying, drugs, women, wine, and all things fine for the last 18 months. I was in the worst shape of my life, aesthetically I had a good beach physique but my general fitness, mental strength, and focus, needed a lot of work. A lot! I had been casually boxing and training but after Valencia I needed to fix up and look sharp asap. Looking back, I was so determined and had complete confidence that I would become a Bootneck, even though the minimum criteria to join Royal Marines training sets the men apart from the boys. Greatness requires delusional belief and I must have had to be out of my mind, but I had decided this is what I was going to do and as long as my body kept up with my mind, I would earn that green beret if it killed me! And that it may, as I had no idea what I was letting myself in for, or what I was made of. But I was about to find out.

But wait, in case you don't know, please allow me to introduce you to the legendary Royal Marine Commandos.

The Royal Marine Commandos are the UK's special operations capable <u>commando</u> force amphibious <u>light infantry</u>. The Corps can trace their origins back to the formation of the "Duke of York and Albany's maritime regiment of Foot" on 28 October 1664, and can trace their commando origins to the formation of the <u>3rd Special Service Brigade</u>, now known as 3 Commando Brigade on 14 February 1942. During the <u>Second World War</u> Winston Churchill had asked for volunteers for an elite body of men who would take on the missions behind Nazi occupied lines, considered kamikaze missions, where men would almost certainly meet their death. He was overwhelmed with applicants. The training was so intense that many would die just during training. These men became so feared by the Nazis and were so successful through fearless and selfless heroics that on 18 October 1942, the Nazi high command issued the 'Commando Order' (German) 'Kommandobefehl'. The order stated that all Commandos captured should be summarily executed without trial, even if in proper uniforms or if they attempted to surrender. Any small group or even suspected commandos not in proper uniforms who fell into the hands of the German forces by some means other than direct combat (by being apprehended by the police in occupied territories, for instance), were to be handed over immediately to the infamous Nazi SS for immediate execution. SS being an abbreviation of Schutzstaffel, or German for "Protective Echelon". The worst of the worse.

Fast forward to modern times, Royal Marine Commandos are now specialised and adaptable light infantry and commando force; Royal Marine Commandos are trained for rapid deployment worldwide and capable of dealing with a wide range of threats. Pirate raiding parties, protecting the UK's nuclear weapons, Iraq, Afghanistan, you name it; we are often the first official boots on the ground. This is why I chose to become a Royal Marine. The honour of following in these men's footsteps was intoxicating to me, and when the shit hit the fan, I not only wanted to be one of the baddest mother fuckers on the planet, I wanted to be surrounded by them.

Bootneck is a nickname for a Marine. Derived from the leather Marines used to cut from their boots and wrap around their necks to stop their throats being cut.

I couldn't wait to get started and see what I was made of...

The Royal Marines Pre-Joining Fitness Test Plus (PJFT+) is levels above regular service fitness tests as you already need to be in excellent shape. A circuit assessment demanding completion of 20 burpees, 30 sit ups, 20 press ups to a beat, and a one-minute plank. There is then a small matter of a 1.5 mile run in 12.5 minutes. Once you join these tests it becomes tougher to not only maintain standards but to always be pushing for better, for excellence. For example, the 1.5-mile run is a team effort 12.5 mins out, with a best effort 1.5 miles required in under 10.5 minutes. Now, as I've mentioned previously, I had a belly of beer and dreams, and had only really got hot and sweaty between the sheets or on the beach in the past 18 months. However, I was a fearless little shite, dare I say cocky, and felt this would be easy. I remember searching for record times achieved of these entry level requirements in order to see if I could beat them. I give myself 10/10 for belief in this situation, however, everyone has a plan until they get punched in the face and I was about to get a double uppercut of reality. And I loved it.

My first morning I woke up early, had a coffee, stretched off a bit and strapped on my brand-new running shoes I bought especially for the task at hand. Fired up with all the gear and no idea. I was full of determination and excitement. I felt inspired by my first 5am wake up, not bedtime; it had been a while. I listened to some old school garage bangers, downed my pre-workout, and set off into the 5am mist. I knew the surrounding countryside like the back of my hand and set a 1.5-mile route using a website to be as precise as possible. I decided to start my stopwatch and would only look at it once I had finished the run. Making sure I gave my best effort. Bolting out of my mum's back gate and down the street towards Forty Hall, I was buzzing, I had finally started my journey to becoming a bad ass, lean, mean, green fighting machine: a Royal Marine. This didn't last long though, as I was only 500 meters into my run and felt like my chest was on fire and my body hurt, everywhere. I became a little emotional as I realised the challenge before me. I was entitled to believe I could just achieve something of this level and physicality without any previous training, dedication or challenging myself to anything other than getting up before 10am after a night of debauchery.

However, I reverted to old and called upon my secret weapon. My self-loathing and anger. I became angry, growling at myself, "That it? You ain't even started bitch. Jays watching you and this is it?!? Come on! MOVE! I pushed myself through the pain and built pace as I used my anger to push me through the walls of discomfort. It was cold and I was miserable, but I felt the internal fires burn and there was no way I wasn't going to finish that run. Even if it killed me. Even if no one else would ever know. I was going to doing it. I reached the entrance to Forty Hall and got a second wind, still talking shit to myself. Growling and spitting venom as I ran through the beautiful English countryside. I began to enjoy the mental battle even if my body didn't.

Crossing my self-imposed finish line like a hot mess on skates, I fell on the grass coughing and throwing up as people passed by laughing and joking, or just throwing me looks of disgust. But fuck them, I did it! I was on my way and had my first taste of true humility and reality. I honestly forget what my time was, but it was around 30 minutes for the full 3 miles. Not too bad to be honest. Only joking, it was terrible. But it was good for me at the time and now I had a foundation to build on.

I picked myself up and walked home to continue my training. I wasn't deterred but felt embarrassed, even concerned that I was so terrible, but as I walked home, I began talking to myself and as I did, I felt my chest swell with anger as I had almost let myself start feeling sorry for myself on the start of the run and knew this was exactly the mindset I needed to eradicate from my repertoire. At the time I thought I was punishing myself but what I realised later was I was fixing my mental health with my physical health. Feeding myself those positive chemicals and learning that where the mind goes, the body will follow. But it all started with a can-do attitude, and willingness to suffer through the pain of growth until, achieving a growth mindset. But in this moment, I was just angry.

I became obsessed with becoming a better version of myself, driven by fear and insecurities I would wake up in the middle of the night with nightmares of failure and celebrating my failure and go running. Eventually it became routine, and I couldn't sleep without working out until I couldn't run another meter or do another push-up. I found myself running through the streets, farmland, and woodland of Enfield most nights and mornings; I became obsessed with not only the results, but the purpose the processes required to achieve it. I had a purpose, an honourable one at that, and although my friends and family offered no cheerleading whatsoever, just mockery at my insane life path and almost hope that I would fail to support their insecurities, I didn't give a shit and was deaf to their negatives as I lost my mind in the process. I was never so sure of anything in my life. I had decided this is what I wanted to do, and I was going to do it even if it killed me. Staying where I was would have been worse than torture to me; submitting to a life of silent desperation where celebrating mediocrity was the only way to see any form of light in an otherwise dull world that to me was and never be worth living. I constantly fought off the overwhelming desire to quit and accept a life far less than the one, I was capable of living. I brainwashed myself into thinking my isolated gladiator camp was normal; creating a cocoon of existence where everything around me served my mission. Music, films, TV, conversations; everything served my ultimate goal. I didn't drink, see friends, fuck, fight, anything really fun, I just obsessed about getting my those Royal Marine Commando flashes. My life would be better, I would be better. I trained obsessively and held myself accountable for every little thing, determined not to be led or antagonised astray.

I wasn't focussed on just becoming a Marine, but what that meant to my life. I wasn't driven to earn the status, but rather the mindset. This was my obsession, to get as far away from my situation and the person I was as possible, keeping the good and excreting the bad. I became obsessed with the process, because once I recognised the simplicity of the process and the literal path to success it provided, I knew all I had to do was remain consistent and focussed on my efforts. I did not need to reinvent the wheel or overcomplicate it. It was that simple. In my mind, every mile I ran, every push up I did, every day I went without partying, or stayed in alone, the closer I got to becoming the person I needed to be to start Royal Martine training. I loved it! I was addicted and the thought of going out getting trashed now disgusted me. Women were only a distraction, and I certainly wasn't looking to make new friends. This new mindset became my life, my obsession. I ate, slept, and dreamt this philosophy into reality. I was broke and couldn't have cared less. Money was for other people in this moment. I didn't want anything I didn't have to suffer for. I was all in. Mind, body, and goal synergised. The results showed in my body and attitude. I began to realise a person is only who they are when they are in the shower, nothing more. Everything else can be given, therefore it can be taken away. But to invest in yourself is the best investment you will ever make.

I soon began the process of joining the Royal Marines and attended a careers office several times in London, but they attempted to draft me as an officer, again. I refused and my training was slightly back dated by a couple of months, which really pissed me off.

One day I was in the office when one of the other recruits said for me to bypass the officers I just needed to speak to the Sergeant. So that day after I filled out my paperwork, I sat in a coffee shop opposite and after the officers left, I ran across the road into the office and spoke to a RM Colour Sergeant, who said "That's great, so you want to work for a living". He took my paperwork, processed my application, and registered me for my aptitude test.

Now the aptitude test wasn't a problem at all. Very basic, even for a public-school moron like me. But the medical was a whole new world for me. Again, it was the weird lady. So, I sucked it up as she pulled it out and I was away to my PJFT.

I finally had the privilege of attending a Royal Marine Pre-Joining Fitness Test Plus (PJFT) at Leavesden, Devon. The official Royal Marine training facility. I felt nothing but pride walking through those gates the first time. I was ready. I think I was more fired up on this day than I was when I actually joined, or when I went to Afghanistan for that matter. I was literally going in blind with no context or perceptions.

The training team and everyone were mega chilled as they are still selling you the idea of becoming a Royal Marine at this point. I had wanted this for a long time so there was no need to sell me on anything. Leavesden is a very intimidating place for people not used to the military; with it's one lonely train station and platform directly next to the training facility gates and tall barbed wire fence. It is also next to the infamous 'bottom field' where lads were being put through their paces. Crawling, fireman's carries, hand to hand combat and an assault course. I was instantly hooked! I couldn't believe they were going to pay me to become one of these legends.

All the lads were great too. Every one of us were there to become a Royal Marine Commando, something we each had already put a lot of effort into becoming and for many of us this was the first time they were surrounded by like-minded men, determined to represent themselves to their fullest potential. Can you imagine the energy? Twenty men all set upon becoming a Commando. Day one. Surrounded by genuine bad ass Royals. As we left the changing room and walked to the start of the run, I felt an immense amount of pride and thought of Jay and Oli. I thought of everything I wanted to get away from and this was my change. I had made my choice, suffered in the darkness and now it was time to prove I was worthy of even attempting to wear the famous green beret. By the time we entered the lanes, just a couple minutes' walk from camp, I may as well have been walking out to fight Mike Tyson.

The adrenaline was piercing, and I could barely stop myself from running there and then. Like a stallion on race day chewing at the bit. It was just a 3-mile run. 1.5 as a group, paced by our instructor. But to me, this was one small step for man, one giant leap for Craig kind. My life was about to change forever because I was about to change forever.

We completed the paced 1.5 mile run before turning around and waiting to be unleashed for our individual best effort 1.5 mile back. That "GO!" was like an explosion in my mind, I sprinted off in excitement but soon got a grip on my mind and felt my pace and rhythm build as I controlled my breathing. I didn't try to race any of the other guys but once we set off that pack mentality set in, and it was all out competition whether any of us would admit it or not. I had not run alongside anyone else so I did not have any reference for how I would do against the other lads, and nor did I care at the time I just wanted to do the very best I could. However, I found myself at the front of the pack in a group of around four or five of us and used them for pace until the final stretch when the instructor screamed at us to give our best effort and we all stepped it up and sprinted across the finish line.

Once everyone was in, we set off to the gym where we completed our push-ups, sit-ups, beep test, and pullups. I smashed the tests and couldn't wait to tell my mum. All the lads congratulated each other and were calling home buzzing at their accomplishment. Those who failed knowing where they had to improve and everyone showing them the respect, they deserved for even showing up. We all fail but many never even try. I called Jimmy on the train home and true to form he was magnanimous and quoted Oscar Wilde – 'To live is the rarest thing in the world. Most people exist, that is all."

It was time to double down on my efforts and get ready for the longest military training on earth, 32 weeks. I went home, got laid and got straight back to work. In fact, I left my friend's house at 3am and ran home. I couldn't wait to leave all this behind. The people, the drama, the monotony of mediocrity and the toxic culture that surrounds it all, keeping everyone in their comfort zone. Now I was going to get everything I had asked for. A test among tests where I would find out exactly what I was made of.

Royal Marine Commando Training Structure

Week 1-2 (Nursing school):

You start in a huge dorm away from the other recruits for the first two weeks and are treated like a new-born, where you are taught to shower, your head is shaved, and you are walked through the very basics of self-preservation. Each day, the curve steepens and our Corporal, Corporal Payne ("Pain"), would lead us through this period until we were handed over to our training team who would take us the rest of the way. Or at least as far as each man could go.

Training is progressive but it's not progressive in effort, you have to always give 110% as the lessons intensify and to miss one or to fall behind is not an option. Recruits often fall asleep where they stand and are therefore lovingly named "Nod-Eye" or "Nods". Training removed all the bullshit of life and set me free. Restructuring my mind and reigniting my self-confidence and self-value for the first time in a long time, maybe the first time in my life now I think of it. All the norms vanished as excellence was the new normal. 100% effort with the new mindset and an unnegotiable. From day one you are expected to play ball. There are no special soldiers or room for sensitive sensibilities in the pursuit of excellence and each of us were forced to analyse who we were and how we needed to change to be successful in this world. Lives depended on it, least of all our own. A tried and tested ethos earned by generations of daring men who refused to give up, who refused to surrender, and who built a reputation that has long made our enemies think twice before taking on the UK. I was honoured to even be there.

The Marines care not for small talk and feelings, lives are at risk, so the pursuit of excellence is embodied by the ethos they ingrain in you over 32 weeks and your career. Soldiers fight because they love what is behind them, not because they hate what is in front of them. The irony was, my friends and family were adamant I would struggle or quit, because I couldn't handle the authority imposed by the Marines, but they couldn't have been more wrong. It was what I had been searching for all my life. The world is full of people speaking without the authority of knowledge, speaking with fear and virtue signalling to just be accepted. Creating a culture of lies and deceit where we lose who we are and become alienated not just from everyone else, but ourselves. Here, all that melted away and was replaced by the Commando values of excellence, integrity, self-discipline, and humility; along with the Commando qualities of courage, determination, unselfishness, and cheerfulness in the face of adversity, and the Commando mindset: "Be the first to understand; the first to adapt and respond; and the first to overcome." Leading by example and from the front and taking on all accountabilities and sacrifices in selfless acts that define what it is to be a true alpha.

The discipline was liberating....

Discipline is liberating when executed correctly by masters, and the Royal Marines are masters of their craft. Imagine being taught by a legit Royal Marine training team at Lympstone Commando Training Centre and being surrounded 24/7 by people like you who are obsessed about one thing: becoming a lean green fighting machine. The culture engaged every part of me from the second I arrived. Home? This was home now. I soaked up everything these alphas taught me about accountability, grit, belief, and humour in the face of overwhelming adversity.

Week 1-10:
Recruit Orientation Phase and Individual skills
Recruit Orientation Phase (ROP)

The Recruit Orientation Phase (ROP) is a four-week phase based out of Commando Training Centre Royal Marines, (CTCRM) Lympstone, and culminates in a three-day field exercise and fitness assessment. The phase includes: Physical Training (PT) and swimming sessions and tests, drill and personal administration, weapon handling, Royal Marines close combat training and basic fieldcraft.

Individual skills

During the first four weeks and for the next six, if you successfully pass the ROP, you'll continue your training by learning and developing individual skills. This phase will see you continue with: PT gym sessions, swimming sessions, drills, weapon handling and fieldcraft. You'll also develop map reading and navigation skills, live firing experience and marksmanship training.

Week 11-15:
Troop and Urban Skills

In this final stage of the initial training, you will step-up your knowledge-building and development further, through more targeted combat training, comprising: General Purpose Machine Gun (GPMG), pistol handling and live firing, troop tactics, tactical night navigation, Royal Marines close combat training, close quarter battle training and Strike Operations (Strike Ops) training.

This phase will also see your skills consolidated and a test exercise take place.

Week 16-23:
Troop and Urban Skills

In this final stage of the initial training, you will step-up your knowledge-building and development further, through more targeted combat training, comprising: General Purpose Machine Gun (GPMG), pistol handling and live firing, troop tactics, tactical night navigation, Royal Marines close combat training, close quarter battle training and Strike Operations (Strike Ops) training. This phase will also see your skills consolidated and a test exercise take place.

Week 24 – 32:
Commando Phase

If you're successful in the first stages of training, you'll progress to introductory Commando training. This will see you undertake: Live firing tactical training - at section and troop level, day and night manoeuvre training and amphibious foundation training. A final exercise and four Commando tests will follow, with your success being capped by your King Squad pass out and the earning of your coveted green beret:

- **The endurance course:**
  You will work your way through two miles of tunnels, pools, streams, bogs and woods, then run four miles back to camp where you will need to achieve six out of ten in a shooting test.

- **The nine-mile speed march:**
  You need to complete this in 90 minutes, while carrying your equipment and rifle.

- **The Tarzan assault course:**
  This is an aerial assault course which needs to be completed in 13 minutes, while carrying your equipment and rifle.

- **The 30-mile march:**
  This is a march across Dartmoor, which you will need to complete in less than eight hours, carrying your equipment and a rifle.

Cocooned in this world of excellence, there is no place to hide your weaknesses and your strengths are exposed as you are pushed to your limits. There are no congratulations or cheerleaders required because champions don't need encouragement to be champions. Becoming a Marine is a mindset and recruits shouldn't need any external motivation to want to become a Marine, you have to want it enough to let go and evolve through the suffering, not shy away from it. Accept it. And once you accept it you begin to crave it, as the results and benefits become like a drug. This is why they say, "once a Marine, always a Marine". Everyone is expected to be self-motivated and prepared to do whatever necessary, without excuse or complaint. Those who are not quickly leave or are asked to leave.

The standard is set, and it budges for no one, as it would be an insult to all wearing the iconic green beret (or "lid") to do so as Commandos fundamentally strive as one to be better every day, in every way. If you don't have a fire burning inside you to be the best you can be, you will never pass training. The bullshit is removed and the path clear, all you have to do is show up with 100% effort, every second, of everyday.

Training instructors are fully fledged Royal Marine Commandos, providing a constant reflection of what it means and takes to become one. So, when I say there is no motivation that isn't entirely true because you have a constant living breathing example who is more than happy to correct your every word or action to aid you in your pursuit of the standards and mindset required to become an elite soldier. I relished the challenge and despite hanging out my ass daily, the consistent steep learning curve was everything I had been looking for. My mind constantly focussed on the task at hand without idol time to feel sorry for myself or to overthink myself into a mess, I was home and going nowhere.

Mentally I found training easy as I had decided this was what I was going to do and the thought of going home and proving everyone right was simply not an option. This was all or nothing for me, so whenever my body screamed and my mind faltered, my one-track mindset would pull me through. I was ready to die, and that mentality allowed me to kill off the negatives and weaknesses of my personality. Because to me it was, a life of silent desperation and mediocrity was waiting for me, along with a chorus of "I told you so's". Fuck that! The thought of failure disgusted me so much that I craved the suffering as it represented me getting further and further away from the version of me, I hated and knew I could was better than; someone everyone would be proud of, not scared of or could get something from, but genuinely proud of. I could hear Jay's voice every time I began to bitch out or was hanging out my ass, it was like he was there with me.

Training is relentless and designed to evolve your mind and body into a synergy that develops a 'nothing is impossible attitude'. Whether it is carrying 150+ lbs of kit over 20-30 miles of rough terrain, staying awake for days on end in mock combat exercises, or simply being bounced from intensive learning classes to combat training and back to classes, your mind is constantly moulded to operate under pressure and to the tune of the corps ethos.

The bond built between the training and recruiting teams is a complicated one as it is like having an abusive father you idolise at times. Always desperate to win their approval and make them proud as they are essentially who you are trying to become. They have done what you are trying to achieve and therefore demand full unhindered respect.

The bond is complex. For example, a Corporal was removed from my training team for punishing us one afternoon and evening for a series of lateness and failures. It wasn't malicious and built character and resilience that serves me until this day. We were made to crawl, carry, and run up and down hills for hours. Any whingeing or weak noises would result in the time starting all over again, so it went on and on for hours. To be late, or to let standards slip was unacceptable as we were in training to be a part of something far bigger than ourselves. We were now a part of something far bigger than ourselves and had to learn this one way or another. The only issue was we had our gym pass out tests the following day and when we turned up bleeding from our elbows and knees the PTIs lost their shit. They asked us what had happened, and we wouldn't say so they thrashed (punished) us with "pays to be a winner" sprints around camp, where the first three people don't run again but everyone else keeps going until the final three are left. We then did our gym pass out tests. My body was fucked, and I was venomously angry but had a focus that was the best therapy money can't buy. We were marched back to our accommodation and my training team and the PTIs went into the office and had a huge argument. Us lads were stood on the stairs shitting our pants as we saw only one result, us getting tag-teamed-thrashed. But then something amazing happened. One of the Corporals came out and told us to thin out to our grots (rooms) and do admin.

The shouting stopped and we were called back to our usual programme. It later transpired that an investigation had been launched and our Corporal was removed from our training team. However, this didn't set well with the lads and we each wrote a letter of support to request he could come back to the training team. It worked, he returned a day or two later and said he appreciated the support so much that he was going to take us for some more extra physical education, as we all loved it so much.

So off we went back to the hill where we were put through our paces again. I know it sounds crazy, but we were happy to have him back.

Throughout training you are tested in landmark exercises that test you on each section of training as your skillsets snowball into what it takes to become a fully fledge Royal Marine. Physical Training (PT), swimming sessions, drill and personal administration, weapon handling, Royal Marines close combat training, fieldcraft and elite soldiering skills. The relentless training takes its toll, but I was very fortunate and only had a couple of minor injuries that I was carrying as we began our final exercise, live field firing. it's vital you train as you fight and simulate the worst conditions possible, and these two weeks were spent running around in freezing, wet conditions that caused me to catch the flu. I was in bits, but my mind refused to acknowledge it as I carried on pushing myself to the limit. My body ached and moaned like a hungry toddler. We returned to camp, and I had one night to get my shit together before taking on our final tests. I was essentially 5 days from becoming a fully-fledged Royal Marine.

I made it all the way to week 31 exercise. All I had to do were smash through the final test and my dream had come true. I woke up the morning of the first test and felt like I had been shoved sideways into a blender. I stretched and had a hot shower, but my guts and body were ruined. Walking to the start line **on the endurance course I was worried:** two miles of tunnels, pools, streams, bogs, and woods; followed by a four-mile run back to camp where I needed to achieve 8 out of ten in a shooting test. I had

112

completed this several times in training and with a 72-minute time limit it rarely took more than 63 minutes. I set off in my four-man multiple and we were smashing it. Faz and I shot off from the other two as we passed through the tunnels just big enough for a man to fit through. I was running on anger and literally frothing at the mouth as I hit the woods that led to the road. I felt the light hit my face and thought of Jay and my nan who would be cheering me on. I burst out of the woods onto the road. I was going to do it, I knew it. Around two miles from camp my body began to shut down and I shit myself without breaking pace. Nothing would stop me I couldn't be stopped! Nothing! I entered camp and made my way to the firing range as I began to compose my breath. I got to the firing range and was told to lay down immediately and prepare to fire. But the second I laid down my world span. The blood from my legs and my adrenaline sending my head into the stratosphere and I could see five targets. I managed to hit 8/10 despite this. Luck was on my side and with a 63-minute running time. But when I stood up, I almost fell over and one of the lads grabbed me. Chris Davies. I held onto his belt buckle as we masked his help, and I went to retrieve my target to prove successful completion of task to my training team. But as I returned to the team, they could clearly see I was in a bad way and told me to stand up straight unsupported and I could go about my day. You have to be battle ready at the end of each of your tests. There is no point arriving at the fight with no fight in you. I stood up with pride and straightened as any good solider would. Before falling flat on my back and shitting myself. I had failed.

I was taken to the medical centre and a jobsworth officer deemed me unable to retest and continue training with my troop. I was livid. How could they allow this? Allow me to get 5 days from the end and even complete the test. I was heartbroken and cried furious tears as my mum tried to calm me down on the phone as I screamed at the officer and tore out hydration tubes. I wanted to rip his head from his shoulders.

I had damaged over 75% of my liver and would need to move into Hunter, a recovery troop. I was devastated and angry that they wouldn't let me continue. I had built my mind into a weapon that enabled me to run until collapse and felt now I was being punished for it, or so I felt at the time. But that is the way the cookie crumbles and the world often feel most unfair when we fall short, no matter the circumstances, but like many before me I was forced to swallow hard and refocus on waiting to get medically cleared so I could complete my last 5 days of training. My bed was positioned so I could see my troop pass by after completing their second test the following morning. If I ever was humbled in my life, it was at this point. After a week, I was sent home and out of hunter after a week because I began fighting with other lads who were in the early stages of training, walking around gobbing off. The sergeant had my back and sent me to welfare who sent me home until my appointment at the institute of naval medicine. I returned home feeling disgusted to be surrounded by civilians and their weak mindsets, I was meant to be with my tribe, the Marines, and now I was sat here with civilians feeling sorry for me. It hurt, it hurt bad. A true shit sandwich if I ever had one, but one I had to get through. I went to the institute of Naval medicine and smashed their tests and returned to do my tests, passing with mental ease and immense physical discomfort. In this moment my mind was the strongest it has ever been.

Stopping briefly before completing the final 50 meters of the 30-miler as is customary, we each fixed ourselves and donned our soft lids for the last time. I had a moment of immense emotion as I realised just how far I had come in those past eight years and in the recognition, I was about to get the green lid that represented my success and the fact I had won an internal battle within to change my path in life. A single manly tear was shed. I then got my shit together and set off to M Company, 42 Commando.

———

Joining M Company, 42 Commando.

An eclectic mix of men join the Royal Marines, mostly because they want to become elite soldiers, others for a path to a better life, and the rest I am sure would represent everything in between. Bonded by a shared dream and the immense challenge and suffering required to achieve it, the Royal Marines really are a brotherhood.

Once joining 42 Commando, the pace slowed dramatically to almost a halt in comparison. After morning training there would be little to do unless a specific course was being laid on as things were waiting on 42

Commandos PDT (Pre-Deployment Training) to begin for Herrick 14. I worked out two/three times a day and continued my pursuit of excellence with the lads at our own free will, eventually representing 42 Commando in the ultra-fit competition and at the Corps boxing champs.

I had become addicted to the pursuit of excellence and pushing myself to the limits, which was a very good thing as it was now time to level up once again and do what Royal Marine Commandos do.

Chapter 6

THE ART OF WAR

Pre-Deployment training

We began our PDT by travelling across the Atlantic Ocean as part of operation Auriga, working with the Royal Navy and our good friends the United States Marine Corps (USMC). Awesome lads!

I was aboard on HMS Ocean for our voyage. I was cutting weight and training for the Corps Boxing champs, which meant I didn't have to get involved with a lot of the standard details on ship and had a lot to keep myself busy; however, it meant I was cutting weight whilst on ship and would also be cutting weight whilst on exercise. Normally I would have just cut weight over a matter of days, but I had been told I would be fighting at 75kgs and was walking around at 82kgs at the time, with not a lot of fat on me after spending all my waking hours bulking and ripping since passing training. Tim our boxing coach, would watch as we entered the galley to make sure we were eating what we should and anyone taking the piss would be replaced or given remedial training. A beasting, during the next training session.

The crossing was boring as the Navy trained and we were based at the accommodation at the very front of the ship so most nights the anchor would smash into the hull keeping us awake. The Navy hates the Marines, so it wasn't a surprise we were based there. However, one night the sea was so rough that the anchor broke away, so we got a nice sleep that night.

It wasn't all bad though as we kept ourselves occupied. To make sure the lads behaved themselves and to keep the peace with the Navy, a tradition called ratting introduced by the Marines. Basically, we weren't allowed to speak to any female on ship, no matter what. An officer in the galley at the tuck shop, no excuses. Anyone caught would result in them having to carry around a 25kg heavy bag ingeniously redesigned with tape to resemble a rat. Taking it everywhere with them until the next person was caught. It did the job and kept us entertained. I hated being on the ship, although we certainly made the most of it.

When we arrived in North Carolina, USA, I literally could not believe what I was seeing. We were greeted and followed by cars of girls holding paper with their phone numbers written boldly. They literally chased us down the highway, flashing us and screaming for attention like we were Justin Bieber. God bless America. Parents and their kids thanked us everywhere we went for their freedoms, and we couldn't spend our own money if we tried as men of all ages lined up to buy us a drink everywhere we went. It was a far cry from the UK where we were not allowed into places because we were military and treated like second class citizens. Even in Plymouth

However, we didn't have any time to play and went straight to Camp Lejeune, North Carolina. Home to the USMC and military dream land that is over 246 square miles of fun and games.

They even had an actual size Afghan village, complete with legit Afghanis, tens of beaches, and anything and everything else you needed. The US budget for their military at the time was bigger than the entire UK budget so you can imagine how we felt. A truly amazing place that made us all realise how small and elite a unit we were as we were far better when compared individually to US Marines, but their numbers and ability was mind boggling, even to us then.

USMC – We were shooting on a great firing range in the middle of North Carolina. Two details: 1. Shooting. 2. Safety Cordon. The latter quickly realised they were in for a long hot morning and quickly descended into naked sunbathing and random bear hunts and trap experiments. Well, two lads were among their Royal Marine budgie smugglers when a USMC Staff Sergeant came hurting along in a jeep, driven by another USMC. The Staff Sergeant leapt out of the car before it stopped, screaming "Are you Marines out of your god dam minds!" Before seeing their camo, laid neatly in the hut was Royal Marine. He simply stood back, huffed, and shook his head, before saying "I nearly shot you fuckers. Dam you Royals are outta your god dam minds! Now, put your dam dicks away and have a good day!" In the jeep and off he went.

Our time at Camp Lejeune came to an end far too soon but after a short sail down to Virginia we were given some time to play before heading back to the UK. The lads and I rented a mini-van and drove down to Virginia Beach to celebrate Independence Day. The irony was delicious, and we soon experienced some true US ignorance but were so welcomed by the majority as we had been for the entirety of our trip. We went drinking like only the Marines do and it was an epic night of lads being chased naked by police, girls-girls-and more girls, and hanging out with gangbangers and throwing gang signs at police who promptly came over and nearly arrested us. Especially the poor gang bangers who the police blamed, despite us Marines being the ones throwing up and posing with our new homies.

Then just like that, our American adventure was over, and it was time to return to the UK to finish our PDT.

We arrive back to the misery of the UK to complete our training in minus-degree Celsius conditions, in preparation for our summer tour of Afghanistan where temperatures would reach 50 degrees. Like everything else we saw the fun in it and despite getting cold weather injuries and being utterly miserable, we had a laugh and put 100% effort into the training that would keep us safe and at our best whilst on operations.

I had now become a fully-fledged product of my environment and could barely recognise my old mindset, let alone align with it. As training ramped up for Afghanistan, I began to phase out friends and conversations with family members. Becoming intolerant of those who celebrated mediocrity, entitlement, and anything else that did not serve my primary focus.

I felt powerful, the best version of me. Alone with my brothers in a world no one could ever understand unless they too experienced it. We had each other and would need each other to survive and be successful over the coming months.

There is a direct correlation between the focus and effort you dedicate towards a task and a task's success; but people often fall short of applying this simple equation. The Marines had created a selfless version of me that was capable of anything because my mindset was pragmatic, fearless, and full of self-belief. I welcomed the suffering and challenged myself on a whole new level.

Before we left on operations my Sergeant Major made us write death letters to our loved ones. When I was told to do it, I was genuinely annoyed and didn't want to write anything, but he told us "It's not about you, you selfish cunts, it's about those that aren't fucking dead and might miss you for some unknown fucking reason." Or something to that point. It was a good point.

It must be hard for civilian loved ones to conceive how capable their loved one had become and what he and his fellow Marines are now capable of overcoming together. So naturally they feared the worst, whilst we could not wait to go and do what we had been training to do.

I sat and wrote the letters with a bottle of Jack Daniels. The letter to my mother was so hard as I just apologised for pages and pages for breaking my promise that I would come back. I promised I would always be with her and would protect her from above like I had always done. Can you imagine having to write that letter? It was beyond shit;

but it is good they got the lads to write these as the letters must have brought so much comfort to the families of those who paid the ultimate sacrifice over generations. Young men and women that die with the belief they are sacrificing their today for our tomorrow, the core of civilisation, sacrifice in the debt of freedom.

Afghanistan

A week later I flew to Afghanistan on a flip-down cargo seat with 6 other Marines freezing our tits off, surrounded by armoured vehicles. As we came into land it became very real and my adrenaline began to flow. We landed at night and found our way around Camp Bastion.

After a couple of days acclimatising, calibrating our weapons, and practicing IED (Improvised Explosive Device) drills, it was time for a short Helo (Helicopter) ride to our FOB (Forward Operating Base) before moving by mastiff to our CP (Check Point).

We were relieving the Paras and spent a few days getting a thorough handover. Going on joint patrols to gain their local knowledge and understanding of atmospherics and the local people. Taking notes on local atmospherics, ground recognition and every other bit of information we could get from them. There is a lot of rivalry between Royals and Paras but there is just as much respect as every good soldier knows, iron sharpens iron.

Proverbs 27:17 proclaims: "As iron sharpens iron, so one person sharpens another". This simple statement has been a calling for all these years to understand that no one is alone. That in order to make yourself better, there is a mutual benefit making others better through mentorship, followership, and leading.

The self-made, elite, winners, and the overcomers among us strive to learn from everything they can in order to humbly construct the most well rounded, proficient, and knowledgeable human they are capable of becoming. Seeking competition and challenges even loses to grow in ways they are yet to truly comprehend. We have to get out of our own way and be brave enough to embrace all lessons whilst having the fortitude and self-awareness not to feel attacked or offended; instead embracing all challenges and to grow. It is important to understand who you truly are but have the courage to be in a state and mindset of continuous growth. Soldiers are virtuous savages who must make daily decisions that cost, save, or take lives and therefore cannot afford to even consider self or ego beyond its service to the cause greater than oneself. The whole rivalry was dropped and despite a few jokes and some fun, the lads got on great and we became sponges for their local knowledge and personal stories of coping with camp life and all the joys of war.

My first patrol. I remember being amped up, this is what I had been training for focus and energy. But after 3 hours on the ground in 40+ degree heat I would have taken one in the shoulder to return home a legend. However, we experienced zero contacts or issues.

I thought this was strange and expected or was at least prepared for contact the second we left our CP, but things would not become kinetic for us for a while. We spent days on long patrols that seemed pointless at times as we became acclimatised to our surroundings and new worlds: conducting sentries, duties, and patrolling, working out and fighting boredom in-between.

Then one day we pushed west with two other multiples to draw the Taliban out of a stronghold lovingly called the 'Beehive".

Two Companies surrounding the stronghold with multiple multiples operating as one to draw out the group who had been terrorising the locals. We set off in the dark and I was leading our multiple as a pint man. As I had done on all our patrols since arriving. Patrolling at night in Afghanistan is particularly interesting for obvious reasons, but mostly for every soldier's nightmare, being unable to identify IED's. The trick is to remember your training and staying calm and calculated no matter if your heart is beating through your chest.

We had been patrolling for a few hours when I came across a trip wire. We went firm and a second multiple took up position to cover our flank as I began to confirm (confirm is a term used for confirming an IED is legitimate). Whilst I was laying down with the others behind me, my weapon by my feet, Glen covering. Suddenly we heard two shots go over our heads, we looked at each other and laughed as our radios crackled and confirmed the direction it came from. They were attempting to surround us. We were being contacted from two positions.

I turned, grabbed my weapon, and jumped over and behind Glen into a shallow ditch, but he hadn't seen me get up from my original cover. Glen began shouting... "Bob you old cunt, you ok bro? Bob!?!". I replied, "all good bro" as I ran past him, he laughed – "about fucking time". We laughed and ran up to a BUND (built up natural defence) line just 10 meters or so in front of us. I paused as I got to the possible trip wire, standing up with a leg either side of it, Glen and Scotty stepped over but AK who was close behind and carrying the GPMP (General Purpose Machine Gun – 7.62, a big boy). His trailing leg caught the wire. We shared a look for a hundredth of a second that felt like a minute or two as we ever so slightly braced; then, nothing, it was a dud, the ambush the main goal. We joined the lads on the BUND line and as we did the order came in to "rapid-fire!"

Between our two multiples we shot hundreds of rounds and even a rocket. I had great cover as Glen and AK smashed the rounds down with their machine guns whilst I scanned. I caught sight of the Taliban fighters pinning us down in our position. Or at least trying to but AK had him pinned with his sporadic fire. As AK went to reload, the Taliban fighter popped back around the corner to fire on us once again. Unfortunately, for him, I was already in position.

I remembered my training and did my job before telling the boys around me and radioing it in. We held fire and secured the position, relaying details to the other multiples as they cleared the area, we were now providing cover for. The lads secured the area and we eventually moved off after paying farmers for their dead livestock and generally trying to build relationships with the poor farmers whose house we had just shot to shit to get at the Taliban using it to attack us from.

It is hard to explain but I had an intense sense of primitive survival and dominance. Good over evil, a protector. Very few people know what winning does to your psyche, it doesn't make you heartless, but it makes you use your heart less.

Despite bullets buzzing overhead and the threat of the ground exploding, the thing most of the lads struggled with today was the heat and dodgy bellies. Madness right, such rugged tough men being human-like... but I can assure you the common perception of stupid violent men becoming great soldiers is a fallacy. To be an elite solider you must be intelligent, disciplined, and proactive. Being able to switch from polite conversation and high-fiving kids to being in 8-hour contact with the enemy who wears no uniform, gives no warning, and looks like every other local you saw that day.

The sense of impending doom is constant, but the lads soon become weathered to intensity, accepting the threats in order to best manage them through pragmatic practices and execution of actions instilled through training. In other words, you just got used to it and were always prepared but you become so acclimatised to atmospherics and the ground that it almost felt like home.

Shura's (A Consultation with locals)

Whilst stationed at Noremohammed Check Point, Helmand, I acted as the boss's bodyguard whilst in Shuras. One day there was this particularly important Shura discussing the prospect of us building schools and wells and all kinds of other political enticing to get them on side. Anyway, I was sat directly behind the boss with a pistol behind the chest plate of my body armour. The terp' (interpreter) sat to my right and the boss in front of me, but he had now slightly shuffled to one side to allow us all to communicate. The shura began and it was as usual, lots of introductions and courtesies, all very normal; followed by complaints about how so many sheep had been killed during contacts (gun fights or IED detonations), and other nonsense. But none of this was to overshadow the joy of listening to them show off about the most recent beating of their wives. Bragging of horrific beatings and worse. Now that was a real treat. We soon asked the interpreter to not relay such information.

By now, all this had become common place for me, and I was not worried about anything kicking off as we had the lads right outside should the shit hit the fan or face external issues.

So, proceedings get underway and after a while of conversing with the boss and interpreter I begin to relax into the long-winded affair, a little too much. I suddenly find, myself feeling extremely chilled. I look at the terp' and he smiles, puts his arm around me and says, 'special tea'. Suddenly it all makes sense. I laugh aloud, causing the boss to look back at me surprised but looking equally as chilled out. I apologise. I pulled the interpreter close, and laughingly ask, 'You mean poppy tea'. He replied smiling, 'The best for the best" (a phrase I had taught him) as he tapped my chest with a huge smile on his face. I was a little high, but totally with it and took great pleasure watching the boss drink his required two cups of tea (to satisfy local tradition/culture) before leaning forward with a cigarette in my mouth and whispering, "This poppy tea is great a boss'. His mouth said nothing, but his eyes screamed. I could literally see both relief and horror wave through his eyes. I, on the other hand, was living the dream. Three months of shit and now this! I had another cup just to make sure, and sparked another cigarette. We had 13 men armed to the teeth out front and everyone inside the Shura are always on best behaviour. By the very nature of a shura.

The shura ended and I felt great as I gave the radio signal to the lads that we are coming out. As soon as I walk out, AK looked at me and tells me I look 'Great!'. Instantly putting it all together, as some of the veteran lads had 'spun dits' (told stories) about it whilst I was inside. I mean they had long enough. Shuras go on for hours.

When the boss came out it was hilarious as he was trying to hide the affects from the lads, for all of 3 seconds. He still wouldn't admit it, but he accepted a little help. I went to join the front, having just been handed back my Sharp-shooter rifle. Instead, AK took a point back to camp, and I strolled mid-multiple. Chatting with locals in broken Arabic and giving them all my pens, sweets, all kinds of shit. Weapon slung, and cigarette in hand. Best patrol of my life, followed by 24hrs off patrols. I kept the lads company as they covered my sentry; I was fine, and it wasn't fair on the lads but precautions had to be taken and asses covered, so to speak.

Baby Sitting an IED

Another time we came across an IED and the genius decision was made to go firm and await the bomb disposal team, who literally took all night, which meant we were ordered to stay firm overnight to secure the IED; an interesting decision but one that was made. Putting the lads at unnecessary risk, and to very little benefit, but what do I know? As per usual, the lads made the most of it as we set up a night routine, expanding our position at first light. Prycey and I cooked corn with locals the next morning and sought water from local sources. Matt Pryce and I covered one another as we cooked and ate on our position. Local farmers bringing us bread to eat with our charcoaled corn... it was amazing food in a strange setting, never wanting to relax or take food or drink from the wrong people. R.I.P Prycey.

Terps / Interpreters

Interpreters and translators are responsible for training military personnel in foreign language familiarization and foreign cultural awareness. They perform written translations, and they identify, translate, and summarize communications. Interpreters, or "Terps" are a priceless asset that manages all communications between us and the locals, whilst also listening in on the Taliban as they plot ambushes and watch us. We need to know we can trust them. We need to always show them strength, so he knows he is on the right side.

Educated and brave for the most part, these guys kept us alive and informed, mostly. Imagine relying on a man whose family is at threat if the Taliban discover his identity, he could/would then naturally trade you for his family. You can't confirm their background, and they are the only one in your group who can understand the Taliban's communications. They could literally be directing us into an ambush, and we would have no clue without the interpreter. It was my experience that these were simply very brave men who wanted a better life for the future generations of Afghanistan. Their children are free to study, learn, and experience a fraction of the freedoms we have in the west. Unfortunately, all these dreams were dashed away in an instant and the Taliban handed $86 billion of the world's best military equipment, as if a sick joke I could never have imagined whilst out there. Oh well, dreams dashed, people butchered, and every loss and casualty suffered without the prospect or result of freedoms to justify them. But no matter the demonic state of western politics right now, the Taliban always said, "you have the watches, but we have the time".

Anyway... back to my story.

The interpreters were friendly but not friends. Some I trusted others I didn't and on occasions we would make decisions as opposed to their advice or the information they presented. It's a ballsy move but every move is in Helmand.

In war all the usual human daily concerns and bureaucratic bullshit evaporate, it is about survival and sticking together to survive and win the day. That is where the bond is earned, in joint suffering and overcoming's. Society is dedicated to separatism, tribalism, and fearmongering to achieve an element of control. Elite teams such as the Marines operate in exactly the opposite manner. Our strength is in our unity; his problem is my problem, his safety is as much a concern to me as my own. Working with each other, for each other, towards a united task. We have lost the beauty of each other in western society today, putting all our energy into fighting each other and surviving the many pressures of societal demands and outrages, alone. People ask how I managed to cope in Afghanistan, but I could do that every single day before I could work a 9 to 5, no question. It is only when we go through something or are truly tested and are forced to come together that we unleash humanities greatest superpower. Community, unity, teamwork – togetherness; whatever you want to call it. Those who have served understand something many never will, no matter what you achieve in life, or the money you make, the greatest gift we will all ever have is each other. Especially when in a barbaric warzone.

It was hard to deal with the open paedophilia and use of the children. A very hard pill to swallow for the lads but very much part of their culture and something we never directly saw but all the signs were there; little boys wearing makeup every (man love) Thursday, and little girls as young as 12 marrying men as old as 50+ year-olds after being sold by their father for land, jewels, or status.

Then, I got a little break. After 5.5 long months, it was finally time for Glen and I to leave the rest of the lads to handle business and get some R'N'R. Heading back to Camp Bastion before flying back to the UK for what should have been 14 days of downtime. Most lads losing a few days due to the RAF Regiments legendary fucks given for Bootnecks, so we got 11 days not 14. Cheers lads.

Anyway... Glen and I landed back at bastion via helicopter and as we were getting off guess who was also getting off, Cheryl Cole. She was visiting Camp Bastion to boost the morale of injured lads waiting to go home, those suffering the long slog of logistical support and air conditioning, and those legendary Camp Warriors we all love to hate. Glen and I fucked off the briefing which boiled down to behaving ourselves or else and went straight to Starbucks. I ordered a Frappuccino and fresh doughnut; it was the best fucking thing I've ever consumed.

We had to wait a couple of days at Bastion as I mentioned, but we were in high spirits despite feeling shitty that we weren't back supporting the lads when we were still in country. We sent one or two the pics above and told them how much fun we would be having whilst they melted in the kinetic desert. Of course.

Eventually, and at the very last minute, we were given a flight and literally ran to call our families to let them know before running back to get less with the stuff we had to make our flight.

We flew directly to the UK; we both slept the entire way. When we landed, I experienced one of the most confusing feelings ever, a genuine sense of fear. A deep sense of fear that oddly enough I hadn't felt in a long time. I felt utterly vulnerable. I noticed that Glen was acting sketchy too. We made eye contact, and both burst into laughter, mocking each other as we did.

Honestly, I was absolutely shiting myself. After collecting our bags, we rounded a corner and as we walked towards the final exit the electric doors opened and exposed us to our families. Just our two families standing there. Glen and I jumped back out of sight, allowing the doors to close. It was so weird, but we laughed awkwardly and walked out to our families with gritted teeth. I stared at the ground and couldn't look anyone in the eye. They were so happy to see us, but I simply couldn't look at them. They cheered as we walked out and then it subsided awkwardly as if an anti-climax had occurred. But it wasn't that they felt we were an anti-climax, nor was it that we felt it to be an anti-climax after months of waiting for this moment, but it was simply our odd actions that made it all very surreal. We had been Royal Marine Commandos 24/7 For the past 6 months and all of a sudden, we were in the UK, surrounded by our families. I couldn't settle. I hugged my family before running over to Glen and saying "hello" to his family. We then went our separate ways for the first time in months.

I left with my family and as we pulled onto the M25 I laughed and the whole car awkwardly laughed too. I was just honest which helped everyone relax around me. Saying. "This is fucking weird! Let's just go to the pub". I had to go home to change out of my uniform first. I then gave my girlfriend the best 3 seconds of life, and we went to the pub. After two beers I loosened up slightly.

I had specifically been told not to leave the UK or to get into trouble of any kind (obviously), but after one night at home I booked flights to Spain and called up my friends in Spain to set up a meet in Alicante the following day for six days of mayhem, before flying back to the UK and spending an evening with my family and popping back off to the desert.

Alicante was just what I needed, I landed with my girlfriend and by the time we arrived at our hotel, all my friends were there, and it was like I never left. We sat in the sun and drank beer, and I openly held a mini question time so we could get it all out of the way. Them wanting to know what it's like day-to-day. The lads were asking about the fighting and the girls how I was coping mentally. Then we started drinking and I managed to relax in this little oasis away from duty and threat for just an evening. We all got drunk, and everyone told me how proud they were of me and couldn't believe I would be going back in a couple of days. It was so strange but reminded me I had so much to be grateful for. Having nice stuff is nice but having friends like them is priceless. These people have always been my fuel, and always provided endless love and support for every crazy fucking thing I do. True friends.

The type you call after 6 months and it's like you spoke yesterday. I had a lovely few days with them.

It was soon time for the dream to end and we flew back to the UK where there were more tears. Only everyone knew I had got through ¾ of my tour and therefore felt better than when I first went. For me, I just threw that switch and returned ready to go.

I met Glen and some others at Brize Norton, and we flew back to Camp Bastion. Grabbed our kit, some treats for the lads and jumped on a Helo back to our FOB where we met our multiple and patrolled back to our CP. I felt a sense of relief, I was back. Strange isn't it.

The next morning the Boss called me into the command tent with another lad and told us we had been selected to join a small team tasked with disrupting Taliban activity in an area of increasing concern and strategic importance. A larger Army force was struggling with the local community and so the powers that be decided to form a new multiple and send us to approach it from a different angle. The area had previously suffered at the hands of a Taliban sniper who is believed to have once killed two Para troopers with one shot. Folad was going to be a whole new ball game by the sound of it.

Our multiple patrolled Scotty and I to our company FOB (Forward Operating Base) to meet the other guys and received a full briefing. We then patrolled as a large force up to our new home. Knowing the Taliban were watching.

The Check Point (CP) was huge. Complete with its own landing pad within the walls. Arks over the entire surrounding area, and a tower a hundred or so meters away on the river/crossing. This tower would be covered 24/7 by a team of two Marines. Often getting contacted by either shoot and scoots (ride by shooting on motorbikes) or by those hiding out of sight from the retaliation of the main camp and its walls where lads would have helmets and body armour on but in their boxers only from the waist down. Wasting no time in returning fire, day, or night.

One day we set out to disrupt Taliban activities and look for a fight. And a fight is what we've got. We had been patrolling for a few hours, it was now early afternoon and over 40 degrees. We were crossing open ground when the interpreters picked up communications that suggest the Taliban were watching from close by and orchestrating an ambush. The interpreters noting their accents were not from the area. They were Pakistani and therefore hardcore Taliban fighters.

We were heading to a courtyard to encourage the fight when suddenly we were contacted from what felt all around us. We peeled off and maneuvered into the courtyard that provided waste height cover. We took up 360 arcs and were on the command of "Rapid Fire!" we let them know we were here to fight as we each fired into likely firing positions or at identified targets.

This group were different to the others we had fought. Underslung grenades were coming in close, and they had a sniper that our sniper was onto. The intelligence suggested they were Pakistani Taliban and had now surrounded us and were attempting to limit our movement and move in. However, all Royal Marines are game as mustard and when it comes time to scrap, we scrap. There is no Rambo or movie bullshit, just highly trained lads focussed on winning the day and making sure we all get home. We had to move. Covering fire was laid down as we worked to link up with another multiple of Marines in a position a few hundred meters away. From there we could take the fight back to them.

We had to run across open ground to get there. Running in pairs as cover was laid down by both multiples. The heat and the intensity of the moment spiking my adrenaline to levels I had never experienced before or after. My heart pounding and senses heightened to primal levels. I laughed as I ran. It is amazing what your body can achieve but we were exhausted as we sprinted around the corner and dived over the wall secured by the second multiple. The lads grabbing us and directing us immediately.

We took cover and firing positions in a small courtyard, ready to take the fight back to the enemy. Snipers, heavy machine gun fire and UGL's were laying down a heavy rate of fire as our Corporal and Sergeant gripped and briefed our multiple. We were to push through this position and flank the enemy, securing a compound as our first target.

We were being hit from a tree line covering our route to the compound, but we were struggling to locate the exact location and remove the threat. We needed to move and fast. Then, like something out of a movie, our Sergeant lit a cigarette, tossed it to the Marine trying to gain arcs, lit himself a cigarette, and then stepped out of cover and got eyes on the position. He stepped back into cover, gave the location to the Marine and the threat was removed. What awesome leadership and morale for the lads. A true leader.

Tommy and I ran 50 yards or so to the next compound, pushing through to take up position on the corner of the compound where we were tasked to keep eyes on our left flank and stop the enemy flanking us.

The walls were around 10ft high, and we were leaning up against them to maintain balance on the very thin footpath that was giving way at the edge to an extremely well irrigated seeded field. Suddenly, I heard a loud bang and felt warm liquid all over the left side of my face and body, my eyes were closed, and I braced for pain and a horrible sight of Tommy who was in front of me... I opened my eyes and started nervously laughing. I could see Tommy was covered in mud, as was I. An underslung grenade (UGL) had been fired in a near perfect shot over the compound and within feet of us, luckily for us it landed in the soaked mud of the heavily irrigated field. We were so lucky. By no means the most dangerous situation but this moment always stuck with me as it brought such levity to a moment among months of mad moments; The whole thing lasted seconds but I'll always remember it. We pushed through to take the compound and then again to flank their position. Taking up position in a ditch adjacent to their compound stronghold. Air support had been requested and our attached rank radioed in to update the grid. Marking it and requesting an ETA. We were told a 500lb was the closest and on route. Whether this was a bite (a joke) or not I don't know but we knew it would be a while, so we found strong positions and let them know we were there with a show of force. Rapid fire from 16 Royal Marines. We didn't receive a flurry back like before and it went quiet until the aircraft could be heard. It dropped into position as if to drop the bomb but pulled out last minute, simply threatening the position. To say we were disappointed would be an understatement. It came back down the line that our Major had called off the attack in the last moments.

We pushed on regardless and through the position and after some intel reported back to us that all enemies had dispersed or left the area. We pushed Norther to link up with the rest of our CP multiples and head back to camp.

Days like these became common place with us being contacted whenever we left camp. Or our CP would be contacted most days, and this was always the lads welcomed at the time. Eager to fight the real Taliban and get the rounds down as our tour came to an end.

As we began to make plans to hand over our positions and return home, the energy shifted massively. It was almost as if, if we are going home, let's go home now. It is difficult to keep your head in the game in most circumstances in life but when you know you could be home within weeks to your kids, loved ones, pets, and normality it causes a lot of discombobulated heads. Disciplined and dedicated but with an overwhelming desire to fuck that all off just for a while to relax and essentially not be at war.

It was finally time to fly to Bastion where we as a company would manage all our kit and enjoy all the luxuries of camp. Food and ice being my favourites. I must have eaten 8 meals a day those first couple of days. Within days it was time to go home. There would be no direct flight home this time though, oh no; This time we had to spend two days in Cyprus for 'decompression'. We even had to take a sea swimming test before we could socialise at the beach. Imagine that! Can you imagine the attitude of 160 Marines post Afghanistan being asked by a jobsworth to do a swimming test, we had to laugh about it and took the piss, but it was a sure sign we weren't in Afghanistan anymore. Health and safety were reengaged. We spent the time getting drunk and fucking around. The mix of booze and painkillers sent most of the lads more mental than usual with the evening's entertainment and two beers maximum going out the window after we raided the bar and everyone got naked, causing the officers to leave as the lads tormented them with strip shows and lap dances.

We finally got our flight time and jumped on a passenger plane. Some lads continued drinking and when we arrived, they had to be delivered to their families away from the awaiting news cameras and other families. As I walked through, I spotted my parents who had come together to collect me, my girlfriend at the time choosing not to. I was pretty gutted about this at the time, imagine doing that. I knew then she wasn't for me. Everyone's family and loved ones were there and super excited, as you can imagine. I just wanted to go drinking with the lads but instead it was a car party. Our journey home was one of the best of my life because my mum and dad were purely focussed on something bigger than their quarrels and we had so much fun and laughter driving the 3-hour journey home. My mum didn't know what I drank so brought two of four types of beer. I was drunk before we hit the M25 as we laughed and laughed as they told me about the stresses of me being away and about the riots across London (2011) where Enfield was central to the festivities. It was surreal but I always remember that car journey. We arrived at my mother's house and my girlfriend and brothers were there. We had a little party and then it was time to scratch a serious itch, so my girlfriend and I went to a hotel for the weekend.

Being home was weird and I was already bored and annoyed with how rude and casually disrespectful people were. One day I went to the post office with my girlfriend to renew my car insurance so I could drive my car and when I arrived, I was told I needed the physical paper copy of my proof of address and banking details. I told them I had it on my phone and attempted to show them, but they refused, saying they could only accept a hard copy. This infuriated me as I knew this was not their procedure, but my girlfriend spoke to my mother anyway, arranging for her to fax it through to the post office. This meant waiting around for over half an hour. The fax finally came through, but would you believe it? Once I had it in hand and offered to show the post office employee, she said "it's okay, I just wanted to make sure you had it". She didn't even want to see it. This enraged me and I was so annoyed that I head butted the petitioning glass and questioned why on earth we had been made to stand around for ages if they didn't need it? My girlfriend grabbed me and calmed me down, re-asking my question to the post office jobsworth whose lack of empathy had bitten them in the ass that day. I went to sit outside but was clearly vexed. Choosing to walk up the road to calm myself down.

However, by the time I returned the police had arrived and when I walked towards the post office my girlfriend walked over and said the police were there for me. We both laughed. One of the officers approached me and began to talk to me. I asked him if they had been called about me, he said "yes"; I started to get angry only calming down when my girlfriend came back over to me, explaining to the officer that I had just arrived back from Afghanistan and the clash with the post office lady.

The police could not have been more professional and one of them very kindly and politely asked me to step to one side for him to have a conversation. He said my actions were not okay, saying I had scared people, even if they're annoying people, and he knows that's not what I am about. The officer said I was banned from the post office, and I told him I needed to get my car tax today or would be driving around illegally tomorrow. I was in the right and although I had embarrassed myself, I should still be able to get my insurance. They agreed.

I went back into the post office where the person refused to give me my car insurance but did accept my apology. The police we're still outside and I told them that she would not give me my tax/insurance, so they went inside and brokered a deal and got my tax/insurance for me. Driving home my girlfriend just laughed, saying she must be nuts because these caveman antics are turning her on. We laughed, but I felt really embarrassed that I'd snapped like that, but it would be something I would have to learn to deal with. It was so hard accepting casual disrespect, the celebration of mediocrity, and accepting lies and excuses back into my world. It wasn't the world that had changed, it was me, and I knew it and knew it was going to be a problem once I left the Marines.

Chapter 7

BODYGUARDING

I was nearly 30 years old, skint, and felt I had got all I was going to get from the Corps. I decided I would hand in my 'chit' (years notice to leave) once I returned home. It was time to take all the lessons and the new me out for a test drive in the civilian world. Spreading my new, glorious wings. I am laughing as I write this because I was so utterly confident and sure it would be easy. I knew with my new mindset I would bypass 90% of those in the civilian world, so felt confident. I had zero connections but knew it was time to leave the Marines to maintain the momentum of growth I had established through extreme ownership of my time, values, and goals. I was hungry and eager to learn. Ready to impress.

I went to see my Sergeant Major who hooked me up with all the time off I needed to invest in myself with various courses. I completed my anti-piracy qualifications as a safeguard, but my sights were set on Close Protection. I booked my spot on the Ronin SA Close Protection course in South Africa and flew down excited and ready to get stuck into my next adventure.

The course was intense and covered a vast amount of information with two written tests per week: complementing the daily physical close combat and operational training. The course covered Prehospital Emergency Care, Pedestrian Escort, Venue Security, Protective Driving, Conflict Management, Firearms and Operational Preparedness. No Royal Marine had ever failed the course, so I was confident. I was delighted as the course surpassed expectations, and I met some awesome lads from all over the world who I still speak with today.

South Africa remains one of my favourite countries. The course itself tests you physically but because of my Marine training I found the physical requirements easy. The written tests were always challenging as were the added challenges of incorporating lads with no military background into the rest of the team's working methods. Despite what military we served in, it was evident who had served as their ability to operate within a team was obvious alongside those who had not. The bodyguarding training was great but mostly common sense with tactical awareness in a civilian setting. Primarily, operating as a team, legalities, and service. Bodyguarding is all about service. The teams are often woven into the fabric of their principles/clients lives yet so subtle that it's seamlessly supports and serves. Complimenting and streamlining lives rather than limiting them. It is an art, just like anything else when pursuing the excellence of it.

We also had the opportunity to work as an ambulance technician to support paramedics during a shift in Cape Town. It was crazy! During one shift, we saw stabbings, we saved a child's life, pronounced a neonatal dead after the mother dropped her on an escalator at a shopping centre, saved another child's life who was having an asthma attack; stabbings, road traffic accidents, everything you can imagine. I even got to learn about the cultural separatism between blacks, whites, and coloureds. Blew my mind and I learnt so much. We saw so much pain and suffering in a land so beautiful. I was humbled by the amazing work people do for others, thankless tasks, and traumas they take on all to help others who can never and likely would never replay them, even if they could. Legends!

I learnt how to knife fight; how to fight on camera, and some very naughty tricks when fighting multiple people or a larger man. But what was most valuable to me was understanding the mentality of being a protector. A new mindset where I was now the sheepdog. Positioned between the sheep and the wolves. I had once been the hunted, I became a hunter, and now I was the protector. My self-awareness at an all-time high as I weaponised my every ability to mitigate and combat. Utter accountability at all moments with no space for a lack of concentration as a flow of threats are identified, analysed, and either responded to or simply acknowledged. I was in love with the concept immediately and without blowing my own trumpet, I was very good at as the logistics, humanity, and impending volatility. It felt like home to me. I loved the responsibility, the importance, intensity, teamwork, and being a part of worlds, most will never witness.

I had a whole new perspective on bodyguarding at this point and was excited to apply it to London and the environments I envisioned operating in. Providing diligent and proactive security services with world class service quickly became my new passion, my new obsession. I felt comfortable on the streets and had a lot of connections. I would build a web of information between my official and unofficial contacts whilst learning the business and building my own empire. That was the plan at the moment. But I was getting ahead of myself as I phoned contacts setting up jobs before our final test.

Our final test entailed the entire class operating as real-time security team protecting Timm Smith, the owner and creator of Ronin CP and EMT South Africa course. Timm, protected Nelson Mandela for many years and has some insane stories. A very captivating guy. An extremely talented, and well-connected man. I bet he would have been a complete handful in his day, and even now. A fantastic protector who told us many stories for the application of the lessons we were learning. I loved the whole team. Former local gang leaders turned Bodyguards, some genuine gentlemen beasts who can serve it as you like and who you would always prefer on your team. I loved it. I finished as Top Student and returned to London ready to take over the Close Protection world, but I had no idea what I was getting into. All is often not what it seems.

I left South Africa but would return for my first production-based security job in a couple of years, but not before all the organised chaos, wealth beyond imagining and being in rooms so VIP, I was the only outsider. But it all started in Houts Bay, South Africa.

I left the Royal Marines on January 13th, 2013. I was now living in a shed at the end of my mum's garden and waiting on a call for a new life, it sucked! My mum was unwell and being back home without purpose or prospect was seriously messing with me but I maintained my discipline and structured my day around getting up at 0500 to run, work and job hunt, the gym at 1400, then back to work. This gave me structure and kept me moving, consistency being key to all success. If I felt lazy or sorry for myself and chose to lay in bed all morning, I would have continued that momentum throughout the day and achieved nothing. However, an early morning suffering gets the mind going and that's what I would do. I got up and I got moving, refusing to let my mindset turn to old. I had sent out over 100 CVS to prospect companies and positions when I finally received the one, I wanted. The rest had been short term, with average pay for work in HRA's (Hight Risk Area's) Like Syria, and Iraq but this was the golden opportunity I had been waiting for.

To be honest, I was beginning to get nervous. Then one day I received a random phone call from a possible employer who asked if it would be ok for her to ask me a series of questions, "would that be ok"? Of course, I consented, and she went straight into a series of odd and deep questions that became more and more intrusive as she went on. She asked me how many times I had taken various amounts of drugs, any criminality I had been caught for? and what was the worst thing I had ever gotten away with? It's a tricky question for most. Had I ever killed anyone? What were my best characteristics? what my worst characteristics were? the best thing I've ever done? the last thing I got away with? and a series of questions that really make you think, who the fuck am I?

The purpose is to gauge how honest you are as integrity is the most important thing in private security. Weak security members are kinks in the principal's armour and can have full access so the process of filtration is immense, when done correctly and to standard. At the end of the call she asked me for five personal references. I provided five names and contact details, and we said our goodbyes. Over the coming days I received a series of odd phone calls from family and friends who had also had these calls and been asked similar odd questions about me; they had also been asked to give five further references themselves, meaning that in a matter of 24 hours they were requesting 30 references and now these people were calling me. We laughed, they were all more interested in what I was up to now, it was another test as the whole thing was, I couldn't say. Instantly tested by the company with 30 of my nearest, dearest or blast from the past. I hadn't spoken to in a number of years.

I received a call from my friend in Enfield, north London who said, and I quote "geezer I got some yank cunt on the phone asking me all kinds of questions, are these the filth or what". I also had friends who ingeniously gave out the telephone numbers of ex-girlfriends of mine; it was nearly not worth it; I mean give me a break. They wanted this job kept quiet and now they were broadcasting it to everyone I knew with loose lips.

It got to the stage where the company had to call me because nobody would speak to them without an introduction from me. They told me to speak to everybody and tell them he would be calling, I said I would, didn't and got a call within 48 hours offering me an interview the following week. Now, this certainly isn't any regular interview, you're flying to America for 10 days. Everything from polygraph tests, character analysis, a mental analysis and then we went to our accommodations to rest and relax before the rest of the training begun.

Stress inoculation. This is a fancy term for testing your composure and ability to function under stress. Things like fighting an attack dog, getting pepper sprayed with military strength pepper spray into both eyes and quite often the nose, or anything typically combat associated.

There were two other UK applicants, a former Paratrooper and the former RMP, Military Police. We were put in the same group and pepper sprayed literally 30 minutes before we took our turn at the assault course; but despite this and my vision being nearly zero we came first second and third.

We had our fighting skills and character checked as we fought professional MMA fighters in a series of situations where instructors would blind us with lights, before pushing us into a dark room where someone was waiting to fight you the second the door closed. That was all the information provided. "The sound of the door closing starts the test". Top tip: Anyone in this situation, move! In any combat situation it is key to move and keep moving, but in this situation, you need to move long and far while throwing a lucky punch into the dark to catch them coming in or deter them coming onto you. The guy literally hit the wall and I grabbed him, we tussled, and I tripped him, but he was big and a beast, so powerful yet agile, so I ended up in a deadlock situation where my arms were burning out as I held on as tightly as I could. Using my legs to leverage his strength until time was called. Thank God. It was a lot of fun and you learn a lot about gaining vantage or using your disadvantages in obscure situations such as this, learning to be comfortable in the unknown and overwhelmed. Also knowing when you are in a situation where all vantage is with your competitor but learning to just fight through. Just keep going no matter what, it's your best option always.

I genuinely enjoyed most of the training apart from death by PowerPoint. Then again, who likes PowerPoints. A necessary evil but one where I have learnt to take notes and stay engaged, as much as it kills me every time.

On the last day I was called into the office and told I had been successful and would be joining a small UK team. I was told during my final interview that it was unlikely I would be leaving the command centre (CC) for around six months as I had to learn the practises and procedures before being allowed to cover the principle and act as the Principal Protection Operative (PPO). Challenge accepted. There was no way I could sit in a CC for months, I would be climbing the walls and rearranging the alphabet by the end of the week. I needed to make myself useful.

For some reason, the Paratrooper and I were put on a separate flight to the the South African Military Policeman.

Then something magical happened, our flight had a mysterious gas leak of some kind that allowed gas into the cockpit; we were quickly re-routed to Las Vegas, of all places. Our flight ditching all its fuel over the Nevada desert before coming into land. Imagine that. A Royal Marine and Paratrooper who just left the military and having secured their dream jobs, are dropped into party central with drinks coupons and a dream.

We landed, I told the Para to follow me as I overheard a conversation between the stewardess and a first-class passenger. We ran from our seats to collect our luggage as we had to beat the first-class passengers through customs, or our cheeky mission would fail. We dropped all the military lines and hyped up the airport security until they escorted us. Even letting them in on our master plan. Brothers in arms baby! As soon as we snatched our bags from the pile of awaiting luggage quickly taken from our suspect plane, we spotted the "other" first-class passengers and followed them. No questions were asked as we handed our luggage in with the rest of the guests and stepped into a Humvee limo. We poured the champagne and were driven to an awesome hotel and given coupons for food and beverages. The poor RMP was on route home alone unaware. We threw our bags into our room and went out on the lash all night. It was epic. Tasting all the debauchery Las Vegas had to offer before dragging ourselves to the airport again the next day, shadows of our superhero-selves the night before. Broken, yet proud of our antics.

I landed home early Sunday morning, prepared my kit and equipment, re-read my briefing materials, went for a little ten-miler through the country to clear my head, and got into bed around 15:00 hours so I would be all bright eyed and bushy tailed for my first day.

MY FIRST DAY

It was Monday and game time! My first day as a Close Protection officer and where better to start than in a £150 million central London mansion protecting an ultra-influential billionairess.

I was laser focussed as this opportunity meant everything to me. Working for such a prestigious company would teach me all I needed and pave the way to a bright career and future for me. If I put the right efforts in. I felt awesome driving to work that morning, I had made the leap from veteran to employed and had every opportunity before me. Many were not so lucky, and I fully appreciated my position, the excitement written across my face. I had manifested my transition once again, cocooning myself from the world and chasing the dream to be a part of the highest level of my chosen profession. I was determined not to fuck it up.

I arrived and met the team before being shown around the property and walked through its impressive security technologies that support residential sterility. Biometrics and cameras are used in the perfect synergy to compartmentalise and secure the property in a variety of different ways to mitigate and deny various scenarios.

I was surprised by the team's makeup at first. Mostly civilian apart from a veteran Army Sergeant Major. My new boss was very experienced, I spent my first week working alongside his #2 being briefed and tested on my capability to support him and the team. The boss of the UK was friends with Tim, my former boxing coach at 42 Commando, so I had a good reputation before I arrived, which always helps as it puts the boss at ease that I am someone he can work with, or at least not a complete, or after his title. It also means they don't have to baby me, which was great for me as it meant I wasn't babied and could start learning the important stuff and start supporting a tired team straight off the bat.

Typically, you spend the first couple of weeks and months in the command centre before being given the opportunity to provide advance or coverage to the principals themselves. However, I was lucky enough on my second day to have the opportunity. Mostly around Harrods in London, little did I know how many hours over the coming years I would be spending shopping in Harrods with clients; one day spending seven hours in the handbag section. Anyway, it was my second day, and I was extremely happy to be out and working directly with the client and her sister. Just a normal day around town but this gave me much needed face time. Later that week I was asked to prepare and support a trip the principle would be going on in two weeks. I was excited to be asked as it meant I had been performing well at work and offered new opportunity. The principle was a dream to work for, a genuine nice person, which meant protecting them was fun. Even flying around the world on private jets and super yachts can be horrendous with the wrong client, but this was a dream job and I wanted to take full accountability and make sure I did the opportunity justice to encourage more of the same. I was all ears and focused on becoming a part of the team. Most of the team were willing to help and brought me up to speed with procedures and client specifics, however after I was requested to go on the trip, some of the lads that had been there for a while couldn't understand why the new lad was going and not them. I understood but it was what it was and despite feeling very awkward, I felt more fortunate and excited to be in the position. However, if members of my team were going to be disgruntled and upset by this it wasn't exactly the perfect way to start my new career. But my boss simply told them to stop moaning and that they knew the score, what the client wants, she gets, so I was going. They were all given specific roles whilst we were away. In fact, many of them just wanted a few days off as they had been working for a long time without it, hence our employment.

I arrived at the airport and checked in the luggage, before managing all security procedures and every little thing I could think of to ensure my client could arrived and simply walk onto their waiting jet. I had concurrently been communicating with our drivers and worked with customs to ensure we would be able to comply with all document requirements on the runway. Setting up the same procedure upon landing and having a direct phone contact with the person who I would call as we landed to enable our awaiting cars access to the runway (tarmac) so we could bypass the airport and drive straight to their private yacht and awaiting crew who had also all been briefed on client likes and dislikes, security, and service requests.

I was quickly learning that security was about control through information, logistics planning and preparation. Trusting your tuned intuition. Security is people protecting people from people; I quickly realised that security would be a hearts and minds mission on most occasions. Where it would be my job to get to know everyone who would be around my client or where they might inhabit for prolonged occasions. I would often arrive at locations and be very relaxed, not introduce myself but walk around and get to know people the atmospherics and the schematics of the building itself before introducing myself and briefing the staff or guests based upon what I had learnt. High end security is all about synergy, no matter how intense or intrusive the required security procedures must not hinder or interrupt the principle, their schedule, or everyday activities. You can imagine how a family with children might find a couple of large purposeful men following them everywhere and facilitate almost every function of their lives. Little things like transport, vetting house staff, post, social medias; sometimes a consequence of and to their fortunate financial or celebrity position, but it is the protector's job to ensure a balanced approach is always taken. So, I was the light and fluffy security, hiding my constant irritation and paranoia as I became obsessed with my craft.

I became obsessed with my craft and becoming the best protector I could be. Professional to the core and studying constantly to improve. My third week in close protection and I had just facilitated my principle flying privately to an island, collected in style, and driven to a beautiful harbour where we boarded a £500,000 a week super yacht. I wasn't on holiday, but this was awesome. I was fixated on acting correctly so I would be invited back on other trips and earn the opportunity to travel more regularly. Even getting my own clients. This trip was easy though as they were great people and very friendly; I couldn't have asked for a better start to my career. I intended on doing this opportunity justice and began to think of how the perfect security detail would operate and the prospect of owning my own company and managing multiple teams. For now, I needed to learn my craft, so I worked every day offered to me. Often being 28 days a month, 4 days off, and back on. I soon became head of UK Medical and created an infant and medical training programme I believe is still used by the teams today.

I began working for multiple public figures (principles) and became comfortable in their presence, managing and avoiding the press, entourages, and most impressively, the ability to parallel park a Lamborghini. I frequented more celebrity parties than most celebs and met so many awesomely talented and creative people during this period of my life it was just fantastically insane. However, each night like Cinderella, I was driving the hour to my shed, a daily reminder of my place. I would sit in there after work and imagine having what my clients had, more so how I could earn it. No envy, just inspired and eager to learn their mindsets and life hacks that enabled them to get to the top.

One morning my brother had locked the back door to my mum's house and left the key in the lock which meant I was unable to open the door to have a shower. Brilliant! I had to drive to the staff house, adding an hour to my journey. As I was driving down to the workhouse, I decided I couldn't live in the shed anymore and I would ask if I could live in the workhouse. I would speak to my mother that evening to ask if she's OK with me doing so. No shower or toilet and sitting at the end of the garden at 30 years old was shit! All I had was work and without it, I was lost. I was lonely on my days off anyway, so I just worked and worked and just slept on my days off to recover for the repeat. My day-to-day had become so intense and all-consuming that any chance I got to just do nothing, I took full advantage. I never knew what my next day or week would look like and had to be ready to go at any time which was something I was used to and from the Marines; but it became a lot whenever trying to build on something in my life, I could and would get pulled away from at any moment. I couldn't do both, it wasn't fair to others or myself. I just had to work and focus on my opportunities as I wasn't paying attention to my personal life and was making all the wrong decisions flippantly with all my focus on work. I mean, most people dread Mondays where you sit at a desk or listen to bullshit briefings about how boring work will be that week. Whereas my work entailed being on call 24/7 to fly all around the world to escort people to televised events, ceremonies, mitigate threats or concerns. It was an insane life. "Hey Craig, are you cool with collecting one of the world's most famous people tomorrow and escorting them for the week before heading to Paris for a fashion show they're attending?" My life was awesome. I met so many cool people. I met so many people that were just what you want a 'star' to be. Charming and as charismatic as they come, owning every room they enter.

However, I couldn't enjoy the company, nor was I there to be a friend. There are a lot of strange and boundaryless people in this world and sometimes it's impossible for someone of status to even walk the streets or a peruse a store without being hounded by the public or paparazzi. Protectors are faced with a scroll of threats that appear in most people's nightmares. The paparazzi were horrible sometimes. But my nightmare was shopping trips, and I seemed to get pinged for more shopping trips than anyone. Requested apparently. However, it was still a headache if the principle was recognised as one post would bring more and more fans until we had a situation. This happened on so many occasions with different principles that we had our extraction plans for each location down to a fine art. A smooth world class service and slight chit chat to reassure the principle that we have everything under control. The full responsibility of someone's safety when there are active threats, and we are wandering around Harrods taking pictures with fans was fun. The level of responsibility is immense, with threats ranging from general harassment to murder for infamy. Constant analysis and planning weaponised to mitigate issues like kidnap, clout chasers, theft, overzealous fans, and violent attacks; all before they can present themselves, mitigating them in their infancy. Most people's biggest misconception of safety in this regard is caused by their unhindered desire to classify people as safe or dangerous, good, or bad. We humans strive for black or white situations with an unease for the grey. This intolerance or lack of diligence in my world was alien. We operated in the real world, with day-to-day people in close proximity to our clients. We had to recognise, analyse, categorise, act or ignore, every second of the day.

A protector must see the world differently; in tune with their intuition, recognising absence of the normal and presence of the abnormal, whilst removing all predetermined thoughts and concepts to swiftly recognise, analyse and act according to procedure. Repeating this process continuously throughout every second of coverage. The hours are long and there is no personal time, with the opportunity to eat or go to the bathroom few and far between. I found this mindset put me in a mediative state, reminiscent of being in Afghanistan. Self-removed from thought and only put to purpose as something bigger than myself, I loved it. It was home turf for me and the atmospherics familiar. Hundreds of different cultures and languages all around, as were other security teams, surveillance, and anti-surveillance teams. All working with and against one another whilst hiding in plain sight with the general public.

One time I was covering a principle in and around Knightsbridge, shopping, lunching etc. I noticed someone walking past who just seemed off, so I tracked his movement. He happened to cross the road and drop what looked like a phone or battery into a car window that was slightly open. Now my attention was drawn to the car I recognised the car had oil haze windows, the type you can see perfectly out of but not into. I called the advance to check out the vehicle and I got a freaky result back. I had spotted a friend of mine who was doing surveillance on someone else in the area who had yet to spot them; my advance said that the guy had recognised me too and asked me to come over. I switched coverage with the advance and went to speak to my old friend (who I can't name) jumping in the car beside him. After a quick two minute catch up and exchange of contact details and gossip, I said not to worry, we wouldn't blow his cover. Although, I did tell my principle as she had recognised the switch in cover and asked where I had gone. I wanted her to feel safe and know we as a team had strong contacts, so I told her what had happened but would tell her everything in the car in private. Wealthy people love that shit. Who doesn't?

It was like a game but with real life consequences. It had to be approached as a game to remain composed and desensitize, resulting in pragmatic process and being in tune with my unhindered intuition. Not robotic, but pragmatic and focussed. You couldn't walk around stiff with worry the entire time, so the application of the corps ethos, 'humour in the face of adversity' worked well to professionally apply levity and a relaxed method of execution whilst on task. I was relaxed in combat and comfortable in de-escalating situations which often occurred everywhere we seemed to go. With situational awareness and preparation always serving us far better than throwing our weight around. I mean, would you mess with two 6ft plus men wearing bullet-proof vests and earpieces, dressed smart as a guard, and looking twice as fucking hard? You would be silly to do so. Those people are professionals and legally allowed to defend themselves and their clients against threats such as you. Walking around London with jewellery worth a few million. Everything from fans to snatch-and-grabs, all for shopping and lunch. You must be on point and consider all options.

One day I had a client insist I leave her world-famous children with the Nanny at Hyde Park and collect her from an office before returning to the park. An hour round trip. We had a verbal disagreement over the phone where I explained that in no way shape or form would I leave the children unprotected. On basic principle as human, let alone paid professional protector. Noting, I could only imagine her reaction if something happened; she would be crying to the press that I had caused the kidnap of her children and it would not only be the children that suffered at her decision, by my entire family too. She exploded and told me not to be dramatic. She hung up and I went back to protecting her children. She called the nanny 30 mins later and asked how long ago I had left. The nanny handed me the phone and we had the same conversation. I told her I would send a private car and have her brought to our exact location. I did just that, ignoring the threats on my job, among other things. A few mins later I recognised a pap and went to speak to him about not filming the kids. He told me "She" had arranged it and had meant to arrive an hour ago. I laughed, now it all made sense.

She arrived and went nuts at me whilst doing her makeup in the back of the private car, the kids defending me, to her fury. They had some staged family photos, and we went home for. A day in the life of a bodyguard is not what it seems I can tell you. However, her husband brought me down spaghetti bolognaise, and everything was ok again. We had a chat and I told him I was leaving so he signed my breast plate, and we said our goodbyes.

I left the company after gaining experience at the highest level and becoming head of UK medical. I had had the jump start to my career that I needed and when things became toxic as I began to be considered for managerial roles, two leading managers created a gay Tinder profile of me to embarrass me in front of clients, so it was time for me to go. Many useless people excel in others processes but cannot think outside the box or excel without attacking others. The security industry is no different. I handed in my notice and left the next day. I created my own company, Fortified Freedom, and stepped onto the circuit. Within 18 months we had several high-profile details: London homes, film contracts, celebs, UHNWs. Business was booming and I was loving my adventurous life rubbing shoulders with extraordinary people every day. I was learning the stress and strain of running my own company and still staying in that dam shed at the end of my mum's garden. I had to get some space. There was nothing in my life but work, supported by shed solidarity. It had served me well, all I did was work, I was obsessed. It was crazy as I worked more than ever but I spoke directly with the clients so could manage everything and establish my own processes and relationships. At first it was easier for me as the teams I put together would work as a team and support each other in all tasks or requirements. Billionaires, celebrities, and even the authorities would call me directly, whilst in my shed! It was insane, but the shed was my man cave and a lonely, focussed, virtuous man, is a dangerous man. All I did was thirst over ways to learn and grow. What were the best operators doing? What structures did the top companies use? I was focussed on learning from the best. I learnt to fix people's problems and alleviate their concerns. It wasn't just about security anymore; it was about facilitation and supporting clients with every little thing. Making ourselves indispensable in multiple areas of their lives. Always at the ready to protect but always happy to help book appointments, escorting friends, family, endless errands, walking the dogs, working with house staff, PAs, whatever they needed, we were there to justify our fees and focussed on providing a bespoke service.

I began doing well; I got my own place in St Albans. I finally had my own place after years of living in the shed. I can't tell you how amazing a time this was for me. I made the most of it and filled it with all the shit I wanted but couldn't have before, like big TVs and sofas, a real house. I started dating a lot around this time, it must have been because I had my own cool house, instead of taking girls back to a shed or going to theirs. I was just always working and so focussed on getting as far away from where I started as possible.

Back to work. One day a client of mine and his wife wanted to go to Notting Hill so drove the short distance with one of the other lads driving for support. He dropped us so we could walk the length of the market but then tracked our movement on an adjacent street, making sure to always be as close as possible. The principals were wearing around £9,000,000+ worth of jewellery on their wrists and fingers and it wasn't long before people began recognising them. Everything was fine for the first 30 minutes, then we were spotted a group of guys who were hooded and tracking us as we walked the single road market. I briefed my driver who parked and followed the guys from the rear before passing by them and taking up rear coverage. The guys moved past us but stood staring at us blatantly looking for a reaction. I smiled and wished them good morning. We both pulled our radio pieces out and put them into our ears, I pretended to radio to the rest of the team, despite it just being the two of us. An easy yet effective trick. He then left to go and get the vehicle and reversed it all the way down to the side of the street, so we only had to pass by two shops before entering the vehicle. I went inside the store and informed the client that it's best we leave. They asked, "why'? looking outside and realising the situation, the boss said, "yes OK, maybe it's best". Once they had paid for their items, I let the driver know we were on our way with a double tap on the radio, and we walked straight out and into the vehicle. Many clients get brave and voice their distaste for volatile attentions such as this but there's no point, it all comes with the territory; I would be as polite and calm as possible and if things ever require escalation, well that's the easy part. But the little freedoms you take for granted are oddly what the wealthy and celebs miss most.

Ironically, the price of having it all is that you lose touch with the many of life's little treasures. Meaning you exchange luxury for life's little luxuries. Those normal people have but forget how lucky they are to have them. Like being a world-famous footballer who can't play football with his kids at the park without attracting huge crowds of people bothering them. Or billionaire's who have all the money and material things anyone could ever want, but not a single person to share them with. There is a price for every interaction and even love, especially in a billionaire's life. The juice has to be worth the squeeze in any situation, and it was my job to streamline and access many of these situations to adapt them to the desired effect or manicure them to my client's requests. Making it all seem organic, as oif awesome things just happen to happen all the time without a team of us running around managing every single facet of their lives. I created situations, managed others, and mitigated much more. Often all in a single afternoon.

I was with a billionaire one day in central London, we arrived at a luncheon she had arranged with friends. We arrived and she received a message saying none of them could come. This was as we were walking into the fancy restaurant. The billionairess was already out of the car and walking towards the restaurant and I could see just like any other girl would be, she was clearly upset. she turned to me and told me the situation, and I joked it was nice for them to give her so much notice. She smiled. she said, "fuck it, do you want to have lunch with me? and yes, you should feel sorry for me because I'm Billy no mates." We laughed and I said, "of course". Letting her know I should let the driver know that I would be sitting inside the restaurant but didn't want to put it over our communications. She laughed and said OK, just don't tell him that they didn't turn up. I was genuinely laughing at this stage as she put me in a very funny situation but was a genuine and lovely person, nice person to be around, and I felt very sorry for her, despite her having everything I could ever dream of.

We went downstairs and had a lovely lunch, barely talking as she played on her phone. A little bit of chit chat here and there and then we were back in the car and on our way home, back into the matrix and how things should be...

The Russians...

I began providing international security solutions for a Russian oligarch and his executives as they finalised a merger involving three companies spread across five countries. Over a five-month period I worked to safeguard the group around the clock, whether in their day-to-day activities, business trips, or managing advances and schedules for London and Europe. This was an intense operation and tested me daily as the primary principle was the boss of it all and at his interesting personal threat level and situation, we spent a lot of time on. It was always and will always be imminent. He pissed off a lot of Russians that you don't want to upset, he knows, he used to be one of the groups now targeting him. Remember what I told you about people you know…

This was about as high-end as it got, a 16-man team working around the clock where even the shift handover for drivers would take 60 minutes because all vehicles required physical protection 24/7, despite me making the decision to sweep for explosives, recording, and utilising tracking and biometric technologies. The boss insisted on full vehicle handovers.

The business merger was getting a lot of attention from all the wrong places. With surveillance teams being spotted daily by our anti-surveillance, drivers, and CP teams. We simply chose to hide in plain sight and conduct all movements bluntly and sporadically to make things difficult, only going into full disappearing mode whenever we were due to travel or conduct business. It was hide and seek with ultimate consequences.

I had a good relationship with this client. He expected the highest standards, and his time was precious, so I was given full accountability to ensure all members of the group were not only protected and serviced but also on time. Being late in high society or business is simply not acceptable. Much like in the Royal Marines, where the term was – "If you are five minutes early, you're on time. If you're on time, you are late; if you are late, you are dead to me". He loved the fact I was disciplined with timings and would know where everyone was at all times. Their exact locations. Spending every day together for months we became close; you must remember most billionaires are the loneliest creatures on the planet, they often have everything, but no one, as people only see the wealth, not the man, and often all those closest to him will treat him as a bank, nothing more. I spent his birthday with him as he played golf alone, followed by dinner alone, imagine that. Well, I understand and will explain more later but it's almost like him celebrating with all his friends and letting everyone know it. He could invite anyone, to do anything, but he chooses to do what he wants, alone. That's powerful to me.

Once the business concluded we flew back to London on his private jet, with my contract technically concluding once the wheels touched the tarmac back in the UK. As we walked from the jet to the awaiting car, he asked me to ride with him back to the residence to meet his son and daughter. Asking for me to speak with them and offer advice to them as they had become nervous in recent months. I was due to finish after nearly six months of working every day, but that's the business to the core and we were soon on our way to Oxford.

We arrived back at the family estate, and I sat and spoke with the family for a couple of hours before the father asked me directly if I would provide security for his son on an upcoming business trip. There were then a awkward few moments where the son attempted to deter the need for security, but his father overruled him; I agreed, how could I not, and a couple of weeks later we set off to Luxembourg, Berlin, and Dubai, before returning to London. Everything had gone exceptionally well, and the son was extremely happy with the service he had received.

In accordance with our (SOPs) Standard Operating Procedures, I had booked multiple restaurants and evening entertainment, ensuring we know the venues and our contacts there would work with us to facilitate. He loved these kind of details as it gave him options when others had very limited. A wealthy man's sport.

Mostly though it was simply ensuring he was awake and on time all day for his busy schedule, entering his room to wake him on several occasions and having his clothes pressed daily to avoid excuses for being late. He quickly became comfortable if not reliant on these new services and requested I provide coverage for a party he was holding to celebrate his successful trip. I asked where he would be holding it and he asked if I could arrange it all. "Nothing but the best of everything, just send me the bill". He was clear what he wanted. I set it all up in a couple of hours. We had two suites at a luxury hotel in central London. One was for the security team and the girls that weren't invited to the party at the time, and general storage or to keep the debaucherous shit.

To explain this world a little better as its certainly a different world to the one most people live in. There is always a holding room or rooms secured for the females who have been flown in, often via Instagram (check out www.tagyoursponsor.com) or professional women hired for the evening. The Instagram girls often arrive acting as a prize or celebrity and are often out to manipulate and get what they can from the situation. Fair play, why not? However, it was my job to mitigate this issue so would brief the girls on arrival. We took their phones and bags as

171

standard; they were welcome to leave if they did not agree to this. Explaining that it obviously wasn't that individual or group I was concerned with but always deferred the concern onto previous women, explaining; rules are rules and they're here to protect the client; further building his status to his guests. If they refused, they would be offered the next first-class flight home the following day.

I can tell you that the individuals I met in these weird circumstances were always my biggest concern. It's almost impossible to run background checks on and with such intimate access to the client it really is Russian roulette. The girls seeking to blackmail, gain clout and generally create a toxic atmosphere, although they were the principle themselves; whereas the professional ladies would arrive, be exceptionally well behaved and leave without issue. Such a strange thing to be involved in, I can tell you. I genuinely hated this aspect of the job, but as a billionaire's bodyguard your biggest threat is often blackmail and females, but this is not an attack on these women at all. Many are born with next to nothing but were gifted with beauty, so they use that to achieve and get things they could never get otherwise or would take them 30 years of hard work to attain. Instead, they jump on Instagram and agree to keep an old man company, often acting as a therapist rather than sexual entertainment whilst getting to live the life of a billionaire, literally overnight. I think the girls win in these situations all the time.

Once everyone had been briefed and phones taken, they were escorted across the hall to the party which was already absolute carnage, with the principle enjoying himself to the fullest, in a robe and giant sunglasses, swinging his chap around as if no one else was in the room. Pots and piles of drugs were everywhere and the only thing keeping hotel security from stopping the ridiculousness was an excessive upfront tip we had paid; money solves many problems.

Our bill reached six figures and the food and drink just kept on coming as the girls switched out and the party kept going as they continue to party throughout the night and into the next day, and then the following evening.

We had gone to a club the night before, for two hours. It was Friday, and we had to get tables and access for an entourage of 37 people; meaning a convoy of 6 security and 11 drivers/vehicles now had to leave the hotel in one giant cluster fuck of a night out. Eventually we got asked to leave as the guests were acting outrageously and literally sucking and fucking openly. It was like a debaucherous roman orgy in London's west end. We returned to the hotel in the early hours and the party continued.

By midday Saturday I was exhausted and needed to sleep. I handed over to my number 2 and went for a nap in one of the rooms of the security suite, it was rolling the dice a little bit as there were seven or eight girls in the room and all were wasted, I paid the price. I had not slept since waking up at 04:00 on the Friday morning and the party didn't look like it was going to end that day, so I decided to sleep. Whilst I was sleeping one of the girls decided to sneak into my room and she drew a giant penis on my face with a marker pen. Running to tell one of my team that the boss wanted to see me. Smooth move by her. He woke me up by knocking on the door and half opening it so he could be heard clearer, he told me the boss wanted me. I went to see the boss with this thing drawn on my face. I walked in and he was still in his robe and glasses but this time with a huge cock on my face. Completely out of his face at this point he didn't notice or mention the cock on my face. Nor did anyone else at the party, expressing how completely wrecked they all were or just not interested in looking at the help. However, when I returned my guys started laughing and asked if the boss had drawn on me. I looked in the mirror and was horrified! The girl was in hysterics and so was my team at first, but this was my reputation in a high-risk industry, and I couldn't and wouldn't be undermined to any degree. So, when she stopped laughing, we sent the girl home. Rule number one don't draw a dick on my face. I can't believe that it became a required rule. I hated being surrounded by such people, entitled people. To be successful in this world you must be a fixer of problems, parter of oceans, a virtuous servant to all but mastered by none, and a professional savage all at the same time. I became a professional chameleon. I worked constantly so my personal persona was so far removed as it didn't matter what I wanted or felt, just what I had to do or what I needed. And my need was never for me anymore. Forget happy wife happy life, I was baby-sitting the rich and shameless and as lovely as most could be, this was all getting too much for me.

It was now Sunday morning and the father (big boss) called and asked where his son was. He had apparently been unable to contact him for days. I explained the current situation and he told me the party was over and he expected his son back to the Oxford estate by 18:00; I was given direct orders to drag him kicking and screaming if I had to. He told me to send a message when we were on our way, then hung up. As soon as I hung up the phone, I spoke to my two CPOs and explained the situation. I told them I was going to speak to the client, but I wanted us to be ready to move in 5 minutes. I went into the party room, and he was obliterated on the sofa, with coke all over his face whilst sat naked and alone smoking a cigar. I told him what his father had said, and that we should leave in exactly one hour. He told me to go fuck myself and that he was in charge, and I was just a bitch gofer for his father. When he finished speaking, I asked him if he had in fact finished speaking; he responded by standing up and stepping right into my face before shouting the same shit he just said, this time our noses were almost touching.

He pushed me, I told him not to touch me, and then he grabbed me. I broke contact with him, but he went to grab me again. With his father's words ringing in my ears, I slapped him hard across the face. It felt incredible. Like spanking a spoilt child who had been irritating you for months. He fell back, bottom lip quivering. I told him I would be back in 45 minutes to collect him. I went into all the rooms and asked all of the girls to follow me, it was home time. I went back to the room to re-brief my team before paying our bill with our VIP manager, I added a big tip. I returned to the son's room exactly 45 minutes later and he was sat on the sofa wearing a robe, I went to lose my shit and he opened it to reveal he was wearing a full three-piece suit, and his moron friends did the same. We walked outside, little did he or his friends know, I sent all of the excess cars away, so we just had the primary cars to go back to the estate. His friends were on their own, his father wasn't paying anymore bills and I quickly explained that if they had any issues they could speak directly to the boss as it was, he who told me directly.

When we arrived at the Oxford estate 90 minutes later, his father greeted us and we spent a couple of moments speaking outside, enjoying the spring air and smell of freshly cut grass. The father soon began to berate the son, so he retired to his room and a colossal comedown I expect. The father and I moved inside and after a tea or two we had dinner in the garden where he began speaking of family and thanked me for helping him with such sensitive things, like managing his son. He then asked me for a favour and laughed as he asked, I laughed too, nervously. He told me his daughter was flying to London from Germany where she worked in fashion. He asked if I could collect her the following week and escort her to a couple of events over a five-day period. I said sure, why not, it can't be worse than a brother, or could it?

She landed in a private jet at Luton airport, via the Harrods Aviation centre. Upon wheels-down (the plane landing) I made it across the runway in our security chauffeured Rolls Royce. A very cool scene. She walked off the jet looking as classy as they come and dressed impeccably. A true alpha female and an impressive businesswoman who hadn't chosen the same path as her brother, instead she was obsessed with showing her father what she was made of and had become very respected in business. I greeted her at the foot of the steps. She introduced herself, as did I. I turned to open the car and as she stepped past to enter the car, she gave my bum a little squeeze. We shared a smile, hers devilish, mine awkward, and I got into the front seat. We set off across the tarmac and were soon on the motorway to one of her father's houses where her live-in maid had prepared the house for her arrival. Complete with all her preferences. Even the essence in the house is changed to suit the family member staying.

We soon arrived at the house, and I escorted her inside. We walked into the beautiful house steeped in English history. She told me she would quickly get dressed and we would leave for her friend's apartment, one she didn't know the address of. She then had a dinner engagement. We weren't aware so could advance the locations, but this was common. Time is always a luxury. I stepped outside to speak to the driver but within minutes she tested me saying to come back inside and I should always be as near to her as possible. Saying, "In fact if you were inside me, imagine how 'super safe' I would be. I still have that text.

Anyway, I went inside, and she was in the kitchen drinking champagne with a busying maid fussing over her. The maid was extremely friendly and had all but raised the daughter as her own since she was two years old. A complex but lovely relationship.

As I walked in, she began flirting outrageously then walked over to me as I stopped and leant against the countertop. She leant on me and then across me to whisper in my ear. "If I allowed you, would you fuck me, and would you be rough with me, please? She laughed. I was stunned. She obviously had been working hard and wanted to let her hair down. What was wrong with these people! I rolled my head, so I was looking at her straight in the eye and told her that I was a professional and dedicated to keeping her safe and protected, even from herself, adding: "But I'm always rough". She laughed, snorting in joy. We became friends right there and then, kind of. She explained that she often gave bodyguards sent by her father a hard time, so they left her alone and gave her the space she wanted, through fear of her father. A great intimidation tactic she had learnt couldn't be expressed to her father as it meant telling the father his precious daughter was acting in this manner, something the father simply wouldn't have wanted to hear and would have surely punished or fired the security and left his daughter to terrorise the next. I now realised why I was here. This dude saw me as the child whisperer, he did, oh fuck. He had the wrong guy. I mean can you blame me for being a little frustrated? Just a little. But she liked me, and I knew that meant trouble at some point, but for now things had settled and we were "friends", something I could work with.

We left the residence around two hours later, going straight to dinner. The maid stayed on site and looked very happy as we finally left. We arrived at the restaurant and after bypassing the press, using a private entrance. I walked her to her table and seated her, saying hello to her friends, before walking back outside to the car to sit with the driver.

Where we started to discuss our own dinner plans. Anything close was our option. But before we could go any further with that genius idea, she called and told me to come back in immediately, adding that I shouldn't sit outside with the "riff raff" and "I was part of the family now". I walked back into the restaurant, and she was sat there in all her glory with her arm around an empty chair. She called me over and she introduced me to her friends again and explained I was her personal 007, so do not fuck with her. They were a group of very nice and very wealthy lady legends who lived life to the fullest and it was a pleasure.

She began drinking excessively and using a cleverly designed necklace to take cocaine at the table. I hadn't seen something similar before, but I was impressed. Whatever you do, be the best at it. She became louder and kept standing up to dance to the restaurant's music and was cheered on by the group as they championed everything she did. It was soon spontaneous club O'clock and unlike her brother she made the calls and managed everything herself. She began inviting loads of people to her table as the champagne and cocaine arrived. Despite the area having curtains that closed, they were very much open and exhibitionism running in the family, it seemed. My messy principle wasn't involved in any of the naughtiness, but she was very much the orchestrator of it all. She craved dominance and was absolutely the boss of every arena I had seen her in so far. At one point she came over and jumped to me and rode me before trying to drag me to the bathroom to do cocaine and "filthy things" with her; she said then we would both have a secret from her father and would be forever friends; but I just laughed and told her that everything between us was a secret from her father but would always be professional, she called me a liar and got back to a friends. Before long, it was home time. A small dinner with friends gone mad.

We were soon very politely asked to leave, and she paid the £60,000+ bill and we were out the backdoor to our awaiting car. Constant comms ensuring we both always knew the situation. Right, home time, or was it? Nope, in security there's always a pivot or one more thing, and we ended up going for a lively cafe breakfast in Chelsea until about 09:30 in the morning where the party continued until we escorted her home to an awaiting maid.

Once she was safely in the house and under the care of her maid, I got out of there, whisked away by the driver. Just when I thought I was free to get some rest before picking her up again around 5 hours later, I received a panicked call from the maid who said she needed me urgently back at the apartment. She was playing with a knife and chasing the maid around the house every time she tried to get her to go to bed. I was exhausted and in no mood, but we turned around and we're back at the house quicker than we left it. When I entered the house, I went into the kitchen and she was completely naked with a knife in her hand, licking cocaine off it, great! The maid asked me to help, I walked out of the kitchen and through the house to an upstairs bedroom. I grabbed a large quilt and walked back into the kitchen and wrapped her in the quilt and carried her kicking and screaming upstairs. Once upstairs she chilled out and her maid gave her something to help her sleep. I was now officially shitting myself at the situation and what I would tell her father. I left the house as soon as I could, convincing myself on the journey home that everything would be ok. I almost had when her father called me the very next morning and asked me to meet him back at the estate in Oxford later that afternoon, and to bring his daughter with me. I was shitting my pants, despite having acted professionally and in the best interests of the principle this was an oligarch's only daughter and I didn't know if she had sent a drunken message to him or called him or what!?

I pulled into the estate once again with a cloud of uncertainty over my head and the thought in my head that this really would be a shit way to go after all the exciting ways I could have gone along the way. I chuckled to myself as my overdramatic mind got away with me.

I was greeted by staff and escorted to the boss who was sat watching his dogs chase each other around his outrageous garden as he sat on a luxurious sofa smoking a cigar. He greeted me warmly which made me even more suspicious. He paused and looked at me, I looked at him and he began to laugh. "Craig don't be so nervous, you are meant to be a man and if I thought you had something wrong, you think I'd bring you here to do something?" he laughed, before continuing. "Of course not, I would simply have the guys make you the Enfield underwater swimming champion". Now he really started laughing, so much so I smirked away the anger brewing across my face as I began to genuinely believe this man.

was planning to hurt me. I genuinely nearly snapped at the word Enfield as I had never mentioned it to him and saw it as a brilliantly placed threat. His laugh then nearly pushed me over the edge. Something I have always struggled with, no matter my disciplined mindset. Respect was and is everything to me. Thankfully, he recognised the situation and swiftly and elegantly turned it into a joke. Breaking into the charismatic yet ominous gentleman I knew.

Thanking me for looking out for his crazy kids and unnecessarily requesting the details to be kept in the house.

He told me they had gone a little wild after their mother died. They were barely teenagers and it affected them tremendously. He had given them the finest education, every material thing they could ever dream of, and status. But they had clearly missed out on their fundamental needs: love and purpose springing to mind, reminding me of my troubled friends back in Enfield. It was so strange to me at the time, I couldn't understand how you could have so much and be so unhappy; it was crazy and began annoying me more each day. I didn't understand the complexity of it all; I was caught up in my own perspective. The fact that these people could give me life changing money and wouldn't miss it was hard to grasp. We were literally from different worlds, yet it felt like I had all the responsibility and characteristics that we are told lead to money, whilst those with serious wealth seemingly got to do as they pleased without concern. I didn't view this negatively at all, I recognised it as an opportunity to view the world as it was which helped me better understand how the world worked under a serious of vibrations and that in order to really appreciate summer, you must go through some winters.

I sat with the father, and we spoke about life until the early morning. He was fascinated by my mindset, and we discussed how a man benefits from being born with nothing as men are only valued when they provide something. They have to prove or earn their value. Whereas women are born as the culturally protected it but must work to keep or increase it. He spoke of how his money had empowered his daughter to become a formidable businesswoman as culturally and socially nothing was expected of her other than to enjoy the money, so she had a freedom he and his son would never know. However, the son's ability to prove his worth had been stolen from him as he could not prove anything that would be attributed to his father. This conversation and everything I had seen in my career opened my mind and showed me that we are all truly human. No matter our status or circumstance.

By now I had shared time and space with Taliban fighters, murderers, gangsters, billionaires, those suffering true poverty, A-list celebrities, royalty, the powerful, and even remote tribes, and had loved every minute of this crazy world where art and life imitated themselves, sometime concurrently. However, most people cannot comprehend worlds outside of their own. But sat here in this moment speaking as equals with a man worth an estimated £8 billion. It hit home and never left, we are all simple creatures, us humans; and no matter our status, blessings or sufferings that will never change. The only thing that changes is our mindset. For example, a wealthy, self-made man's mindset means he is more likely to lose everything and earn it again. Whereas someone who started off in the very same situation as him but never achieved the wealth or status of the first man who was (hypothetically) gifted his money. The reason is we don't understand or respect what suffering we haven't experienced. Gratitude becomes entitlement. They are both from the same circumstance. The difference is mindset and the lessons the first man gained through struggle and a guided deluded belief, is that he can become something better, something he had never been before, someone he had never been before. This is a lesson everyone reading this should write down and repeat to themselves daily as I can guarantee you, you are capable of achieving everything you dream of, and more than capable of achieving nothing too. It is literally up to you.

Struggle breeds greatness. Most will never understand this but the greatest joys I have ever had are from overcoming and achieving things I never thought possible. It gives you an unrivalled sense of self-worth and purpose that feeds your soul. The more time I spent with elite mindsets, the more I realised my mindset was worth far more than money. I was far richer than the son of my client ever could be. He knew no struggle, just the constraints of the ivory tower he was born into. He reminded me of some of my loser friends from Enfield. They simply never tried to change their situation because they refused to admit that it all started and ended with them. That no one was coming to save them and that we all define our own path in this life.

With this lesson burning the fat from my soul and any residue of victimhood from my character, I began thinking of what I could really achieve in life if I put my mind to it. Who did I really want to be? What did I want to do? I decided to turn down the opportunity to protect the family full-time. I decided to move onto something a little more fun and challenging. I wanted a legitimate challenge that benefited me. No more adult-sitting or red carpets for now, I needed something to get my teeth into.

That challenge would come sooner and greater than I could ever have imagined.

Chapter 8

SURVEILLANCE

Even the wildest of antics eventually become normalised, if not boring. I was fussing over eccentric or erratic, and dramatic bullshit for a living at this point, I missed high risk security, and was desperate for a new challenge despite my company going from strength to strength. I had not set out to build a massive company, I just wanted to do cool shit and travel for pleasure, not duty. Maybe even get laid from time to time. It had been a while. All I did was work, literally.

One morning I unceremoniously collapsed at a gym and by the time I came around the paramedics were on site. I worked myself into the ground, quite literally. The combination of stress and no sleep finally got to me. I hadn't slept for more than two hours in over a year. Most of that was split into 90-minute segments where my phone would wake me to tend to one problem or another.

I was blessed with opportunities and had taken them whenever presented. However, my adventurous soul needed feeding, and I needed to be tested. I spent all my time managing things and had lost the passion that once fuelled my ambition. I'm obsessed with becoming the best version of myself and when I feel I have something on lock, I look to elevate myself and my skillset. Professionally speaking, of course. Then one night I got everything I had been praying for.

I sat at home with my two Macs open, tracking my teams and answering their messages as I attempted to watch UFC. Then I received a random phone call that would lead to me entering surveillance at the highest level, literally overnight. A friend of mine had been away on operations with a company utilised by Interpol to find and surveil the world's most wanted. Extremely challenging and interesting stuff. Human traffickers, mafioso, the infamous, child abductions and recovery, and every other top level professional criminal that was unfortunate enough to step into a global web of tradecraft.

Tradecraft is a combination of techniques, methods, and technologies used in surveillance. The tools for each mission - disguises, cameras, listening devices and some very cool James Bond shit at times – dependent on the assignment. Understandably, my friend was burnt out and his wife was understandably over him being away for months at a time, only to return stressed and burnt out until it was time to go back to work. We knew each other from the Ronin Close Protection course and had stayed in touch sporadically but him calling so late.

It was odd. I answered and he sounded miserable, which alarmed me. We chit chatted quickly, and I told him what I was up to. Explaining I needed a change as I was bored shitless. He laughed and said he felt the same. He told me he was desperate to get back to the UK for his family. The timing was perfect, so I said, "Fuck it mate, come and TL [Team Leader] my team for me and I will jump on your detail?". He asked me if I was serious and I said, "Why not?". He knew two of my lads well, so knew my team would be happy to have him. They likely needed a break from me anyway. I offered him a role I was due to cover but asked in return if there was an opportunity for me to step into his position and gain experience working with some of the world's best agents and operatives. He said he would make a call and get back to me. He called back 15 minutes later and asked me to be at an address in the city of London the following morning.

I felt a surge of excitement and renewed focus I hadn't felt in a long time. I had been on cruise control after feeling I had achieved all I wanted in Close Protection. My brain firing up and running through all the scenarios I might be put through the following day and beyond. I excitedly repacked my grab bag, switching out passports, med kits, and gadgets to best prepare for any tasking I could envision. I called every member of my team to update and brief them before going for a run to clear my head. I then ate my weight in steak and vegetables and went to bed.

I woke up at 5am and went for a long run to clear my head and own my morning. Knowing I suffered an early run in the rain under my own discipline whilst others slept gave me that extra savage feeling where I would win the day. Something I have always done and can't recommend enough. Earn your self-belief, don't fabricate it. Work whilst they're sleeping, it's the best mental vantage you can give yourself. Paying your dues and being disciplined fills you with the knowing that you have owned your shit and proven you can do something you didn't want to do but suffered through it anyway to gain the benefit and vantage of investing in yourself whilst others slept. Literally, or just sleeping on their goals and dreams. You have earned value by doing something you didn't want to do, but did it like you loved it, benefiting physically and mentally. The person that goes to the gym everyday no matter how they feel, will always beat the person who goes to the gym when they feel like it. Going to the gym is always beneficial to your physical and mental health. Not going is equally a choice, a decision. Going to the gym or working out and suffering through choice in search of growth gives you genuine confidence in your own ability. Literally making you a happier, more confident, calmer, and even a kinder person as you are comfortable in your own skin and accountable of your situation, therefore more tolerant to others. Motivation isn't real, discipline is real. Motivation is a good jump-starter, but consistency is required through pragmatic discipline. That is the mentality of not just elite operators, but everyone at the top.

I arrived at the interview early and made sure I found the company office before retiring for a coffee nearby. I returned to the office five minutes before my interview and was greeted by a very articulate and engaging man around my age. He sat me in a bare office and told me the man I had spoken to the night before would be in shortly. Minutes later he entered the room, asking me to follow him. He was extremely talkative and asked lots of personal rapid-fire questions as we exited the office, entered the lift, and exited at ground level. Passing security and exiting the main building. I knew what he was doing. He wanted to see if I could be 'interviewed' whilst concurrently taking notes on my surroundings. He intended to quiz me to access my awareness and observation skills. Extremely difficult even when you know what the game is, as you cannot let on you are actively looking and I needed to engage him as this was framed as a chit chat interview. Eye contact was tricky and fluctuating to say the least. I had to be two people at the same time. We went into a Starbucks and grabbed a coffee; he stopped talking once inside. When we left Starbucks, he asked me what my favourite thing about coffee was. I said, "it's an unassuming weapon and keeps me alert at the same time". He laughed and asked me what the toilet door code was in Starbucks and how many staff were in the cafe? I told him the correct answers and he laughed, "too easy. How many security personnel did we pass as we exited the main lobby, not including regular staff and what was the only minibus VRN (vehicle registration number) outside?" Now I swear to you, the only five things I had noted were those two, the two Starbucks details he had asked for and the number and as much of the A-H (details) of people we had walked past. I was correct and he was happy. He asked me if I had family, I told him I had no dependents or anyone that relied on me. This had become true by this point as my mum had retired to Spain. I was a yes man, I told him I was good to go and had my passport and grab-bag with me. We laughed and he took the piss out of me for being so keen, but clearly loved it. He asked if I wanted to shadow him to Paris and link up with an active team. I didn't even bother to play it cool, "Of course", I said. I was like a kid entering his first James Bond movie, with a legit 007 as my guide, or so I told myself; the guy was super intelligent, spoke several languages and being able to support and shadow him was exactly what I had been looking for. It was awesome!

Surrounded by people levels above me meant I was again the small fish in a whole new pond and had the opportunity to sharpen my iron against people levels if not universes above me. I couldn't have asked for more. I was so eager to learn as the more I learnt the more I realised just how little I knew about the 'real world'. I wanted to see what I was made and couldn't wait to link up with the team.

He stepped away for business whilst I went to speak with my team to confirm I would be off comms for the foreseeable future, and they were expected to all step up, with pay to match. Security and surveillance come with heavy and unforgiving accountability, long hours and complex tasks that require you to work as a tight team of professionals where personal issues and frictions don't come into it as we are all a part of something bigger than ourselves; lives are literally at risk. This was a whole new level and world for me, and I was mentally ready for anything. Within an hour we were on the train.

We arrived in Paris and met up with the team in a café. Two of the small teams sat separately as counter surveillance. We provided two bags of tech and essential Haribo morale before heading to a safe house provided by local intelligence services. A casual professional courtesy between private companies working under the umbrella. We spoke freely and I was briefed and back briefed about the operation and the five concurrent operations that were entwined with ours. One couldn't move without the other and any exposure or issues could butterfly effect and not only ruin years of hard work but put countless lives in danger.

Being invisible always came before gaining intel. I was already completely hooked, to me this was James Bond shit, but I kept my external cool and challenged my nervous excitement into learning from everything and everyone around me.

You learn so much from people like this. Just being around them is a gift of a lesson you'll not forget, I promise you. The way they carry themselves in different situations so effortlessly, slipping into roles and accents; their interactions, what they value, how they are stoic unless acting to task, and scariest of all, their incredible ability to read situations and people. Gaining the vantage and sometimes predictability of situations and even other thought processes. A lot of it is teachable but you have to be a particular student. An overactive brain-taught process seemed to be the common theme.

I was given my individual objectives and after our final group meeting, we separated, and I was provided a hotel, scooter, and locations to frequent over the coming days whilst acting as a tourist as I searched for people and vehicles. I saw a whole new side to Paris as I bopped around eating and obsessing over VRNs plate as I repeated it over and over in my mind, almost as a subconscious theme tune to my activities.

Over the following days I was a tourist obsessed with a single part of the city. All day and night, until one night when I was eating, overwatching a cross section and was contacted as the brief said I might be. I was told to be outside my hotel in 45 minutes, to leave the scooter keys in my room and to collect a package from a hotel not far from my own. I was picked up by one of the teams and told we were heading south as information suggested our target was on the move. We drove throughout the night and set up before hiring a new car to drive around the local area and secure multiple hotel rooms beneficial to our tasking. By morning we were set. I realised the secret was being casual and simply enjoying your surroundings when in public, as a tourist would. Hiding in plain sight is never suggested as it is often not worth the risk, but other times it's necessary. You might get one opportunity to be spotted, as twice is never considered coincidence at this level of paranoia. Therefore, sometimes it's best to be overt with assets or short and sharp in operation. In and out or even in passing.

We weaponised people around the targets, particularly females close to targets, gaining information, locations, and times as our female operatives linked in with them via social medias, posing as friends. Using coded comments or draft emails in shared accounts to avoid basic lines of investigation or anti-surveillance. The compensated or coerced females would be living their best lives, experiencing the benefits of a luxury lifestyle, travelling the world, whilst destroying the hand that feeds them. But all is fair in love and war. If we were caught at certain points of this operation, we would have been fucked. So, using outside sources to buffer our association was vital. I was also hired in this manner, as was everybody else. Deniability to protect the source.

There hadn't been a confirmed sighting of our target for several weeks, yet his communications were giving us clues to follow, despite often being a couple of steps behind. Things would go quiet, and we would not hear things for days as we relentlessly maintained all searches and operations. meticulously executing our tactics changing batteries in vehicles and remaining proactive day and night in order to get any kind of information that might lead to the whereabouts of our target. One morning I was eating breakfast in a café I had begun to frequent, a complete shit hole that the target would never go anywhere near and somewhere I felt I could relax, at least to a degree. My colleague called me and told me to wait outside the café and he would be there to collect me. We had received information from one of our assets that our guy was heading to Monaco to board a yacht, one we already had eyes on via another team.

It was clear the hosts had been briefed on communications a all theirs ceased 48 hours prior to the proposed meeting. After all, it 'wasn't just the legitimate authorities that were tracking them, other criminals were forever chasing this individual as part of the very business we were trying to disrupt. Our aim was to arrive in Monaco and gain as much information as we could before they departed the port. We arrived in Monaco, walked outside of the airport and the contact arrived to collect us, taking us directly to pre-determined and secured location, the overlooked the poor and gave us all the vantage we could possibly have asked for. I was then told to go out and buy myself a suit and make friends with some beautiful girls and invite him for dinner and the casino that evening as we required soft cover to help us blend in as we searched for our target.

I was literally living in dreamland as I went to buy myself a beautiful suit before going on the mission of a lifetime to find beautiful women to take out that evening as my dreams appeared to be coming true, I felt just like James Bond. Now I mean this from a professional standpoint not an egotistical one, but I have never struggled to get females and if I want you to like me then I can get you to like me. A lifetime of service empowered this little trick. I felt made for this as I walked through the famous square to where all the gorgeous girls always posed and waiting to find the next meal ticket. However, today the benefits would be more than mutual and within 30 minutes I had four beautiful and articulate women ready to meet us at 2100 hours for dinner and delights.

I returned to our safe house to align with my colleague who asked to see my suit before reminding me I had to go out and find our soft cover. I told him I had already managed to get us dates for that evening, and they were perfect in personality and presentation. Noting that one of them had WhatsApped me several times since, leaving them to express their interest in me personally and leaving him to his own devices. The plan was that I would manage the assets and keep them engaged to ensure that our cover was secure as I made friends with staff, waiters', barman, other guests, and anyone else I could in order to present ourselves as just two rich men out having a great time, very much the normal Monaco. Allowing him to manage all communications with our team and any and all field craft that might be required that evening. It was vital we both had our own roles and equally as vital we understood each other's completely, at any time we might need to intersect or overlap; possibly even take over from one another should the situation require.

Whilst at dinner later that evening I spotted our asset leaving the hallway leading from the private rooms downstairs; she was walking to the common area bathrooms. This was extremely clever of her as she could simply say she was lost and using the bathroom to anyone who saw whilst giving us a sign that they were in the vicinity and had something. My colleague left the table announcing he was going to the bathroom and two of the girls said they would also like to go, so he escorted them. His timing was off by his efforts to escorts the girls in a gentlemanly fashion but as he reached the bathroom our girl exited and slipped him something. The phone we had given her. My colleague went into the bathroom and retrieved the information we required before leaving the bathroom and handing it to a waiter, saying he had just found it outside the bathrooms believing that someone had lost it. He didn't return to our table and said he wasn't feeling well which was code for why we needed to get the fuck out of there. I guess my Casino Royale moment would have to wait, as I made light of him but explained to the girls I would remain with them at dinner but would leave the casino for another night, so we could all go together. My colleague left and unbeknownst to me went to the safe house and prepared for us to bug out. I dealt with the bigger problem of separating myself from the females we had invited with us, but there was one girl who was interested in me and wanted to come back to more room with me. I had said goodbye to the other girls and walked off but she began to make a scene directly outside the restaurant, claiming I was married or had a girlfriend or something was going on and she made such a scene now I actually took her to a hotel room upstairs from the restaurant in which we were currently stood outside. I gave her the attention she needed before waiting for her to fall asleep and leaving to meet my colleague at the safe house as planned.

When I arrived, he wasn't happy with my delay, but I explained the situation and he supported me in my decision to leave things on good terms and tie up loose ends to avoid further complications. He then explained the information we received on the phone had suggested they were not vacationing or looking to escape or avoid us or enemies on the yacht but instead they had a meeting on the yacht the following day where no female guests or any outsiders were allowed. We knew this is what we had been waiting for and that everything that he had told us was bullshit as this wasn't how our target functioned. What this indicated to us was he was about to bug us out again and the reason we were also bugging him out was to switch locations and brief our team to monitor all vehicle helicopter airports as well as port exits over the next 48 hours. Once we passed this information up, we were advised that a 12-man team would soon be enroute to replace us, which meant that we would be reassigned and after waiting all day for the call was on the first flight out of Monaco the following morning.

My journey was long from over. My superiors loved me and as I was young hungry, and I said yes to absolutely every single opportunity they offered me, so I began to be offered some extremely challenging tasks that gave me an amazing insight into true criminality and how this world affects the world we know. How governments, politicians, and people of influence must be corrupted if not instigators for these activities to be prided the sanctuary to become so prominent. Criminality is entwined in the foundations of every society.

Many people in this crazy world are well over their head and find themselves in situations because of their skillset or position of power. Not because they wanted to enter the criminal world. They are coerced or threatened. So, people have security to deter intimidation, blackmail etc. But when you reach a certain level, it's advised to have anti-surveillance operations as a separate team. Providing an overview and support coverage with all eyes on deck but protectors have a primary duty to focus and recognise immediate threats. Surveillance adds another level of consideration and ability is always being tested so must always be under consideration for improvements.

A dedicated career criminal affects his entire family and everyone they meet once on some level. Imagine eight armed men storming your house and dragging your mother and father out onto the front lawn in front of all your neighbours, hogtying them before masked men take your children to social services, kind of illegally hiding the children for leverage. I have seen that both sides of the criminal world and crime really doesn't pay. However, this form of manipulation and blackmail works on many levels. It is not about punishment; at this level it is about information and most people start talking to authorities immediately. They recognise that their criminal colleagues will likely be concerned they will talk and begin intimidation tactics, so a favoured trick is for authorities to go through proceedings and sentence the individual to serious time in prison, only to let them out the back door of the prison a few weeks later. Releasing them into a witness protection programme with a new identity and life for them and their family.

I was learning from the best once again and became close with a lot of the people I worked with. A unique unity like serving in the Marines, where only those who have done it or where there can really understand what it is like or understand what it takes to operate at this level for prolonged periods. You have to be 100% in, no off or sick days. I found constant motivation to excel and reach my full potential by the great examples set all around me. All I had was effort and interest and those who had been in the game were more than willing to show me the ropes because of it. A disciplined, alpha mindset was fundamental to my success, not just professionally, but in my personal life too. Forming habits that helped form self-belief and confidence that in turn gave me the confidence to be open enough to learn under pressure with humility, knowing I didn't know everything and that there was plenty of room for improvement, but armed with the knowing that if I remained disciplined, positive, and humble, I could learn what I needed to become consistently good enough to operate at the highest level. Being great is great, but it is better to be good all the time rather than great on occasion but bad for the most part. Consistency is key as it forms habits, rituals, and eventually your character. We are what we repeatedly do, and once we build consistency, we gain momentum, and once we gain momentum, we find ourselves 'in the zone'; open, tolerant to all concepts and eventualities, trusting our intuition and creating a new standard for ourselves that will enable us to achieve things we once couldn't. Sounds simple, but the devil is in the accountability.

I had proven my dedication and accountability to standards and task. I received a call one day from my boss who asked if I fancied a challenge with the big boys. I was already excited and said yes before he told me the exact details of the tasking. He loved my enthusiasm but explained I would be heading east and operating within a two-man team pursuing a Mafia paymaster general who operated directly with the mafia bosses to distribute laundered funds throughout the organisation. This was an extremely sensitive detail, and we would be working directly with high level operatives from multiple countries and supported from high up on high.

I landed in country two days later and made myself busy looking like a tourist as were my instructions until contacted and given further instructions, simple. A couple of days later my colleague collected me and I was taken to multiple safe houses and locations and given a full in-depth briefing. I would be operating solo at certain stages due to the necessity of the task and was shown how to set up multiple tradecraft support systems and high-level surveillance techniques, such as setting up a car to make it look like a family vehicle, but actually had more cameras than any red-carpet event I had ever seen. Also, I was show how to maintain and change the batteries for these camera systems to ensure we captured everything always and I was also introduced to some new tagging and tracking equipment that made me really feel like I had entered a James Bond film. My first inclusion within the team was to physically track and surveil family members associated with our primary target but then it was time for us to retag (put new trackers in the) vehicles and begin to tighten the net around our target.

One night we received information that he would be travelling to another country and were unsure of the reason behind it. However, we knew we had to retag his vehicle as following anyone over long distances using line of sight is not feasible and certainly not advised. That night we knew where he would be, and I was tasked with changing the tag. We had information and devices providing us real-time date and surveillance so were able to listen to their conversations and choose the perfect moment for me to slide underneath the vehicle outside the front of the premises and tag the vehicle. When tagging a vehicle, it is important to understand that the tag itself is a small cylinder shape that is about a thick as a UK 2 pence coin or US quarter and roughly around 10 centimetres long; and the way in which it sticks to the vehicle is that you place it underneath inside the bumper of the vehicle, under the internal lip, where you can stick it internally within the curvature of the bumper itself, which makes it very hard to find unless you're looking for it or using high-tech scanners. My colleague and I were in radio communications, and he talked me through the targets movements as I slid underneath the car and retrieved the old tag from the bumper. As I placed it in my pocket and withdrew the new tracker my earpiece crackled very quietly and my colleague said the terrifying words "go firm, he's out (of the house)". I could not believe what I was hearing but slid underneath the vehicle as best I could, leaving a couple of inches of my left shoulder exposed on the slanted driveway as he entered the vehicle and I heard him rummaging in what sounded like the glove box, I just prayed that he did not start the car. My colleague and I obviously did not speak during this time, and it is only once he stepped back out of the vehicle, reset the car alarm, and entered the house; that I began breathing again. Rolling from under the car and into cover as we had planned, and I had entered the position in the first place. Then I casually walked to the end of the street, turned right, and began walking before my colleague collected me and we drove off into the night where I needed to change my underpants, metaphorically speaking of course.

We then spent the next month tracking him and his colleagues around three countries. It was by far the best detail and mission I have ever been involved with but cannot comment on this further as I would breach serious legal boundaries clearly defined to me whilst writing this book.

I returned home after months away, sleeping like a baby for the first few days before catching up with a girl I had been seeing at a luxury country spa for a long weekend, heaven on earth. Laying there the morning we were due to leave, my phone began ringing with the name of a very powerful man, I knew it was time to go back to work.

I answered the phone and stepped out on to our terrace, what he told me was insane, I have heard and seen some things, but this genuinely scared me, it was disgusting but the timing was perfect as I had a whole new bunch of contacts that could help me out.

Here is what happened. It is something that exists at the foundation of most societies across the world and the best kept secret from the public. Although Epstein brought things near to the surface, the powerful are self-policed and governed, so even I would never speak on some of the things I have heard, only my personal experiences, my truth. No names or profiting off other names and efforts, just my story and how all this crazy shit shaped me.

My client explained that his son was studying at a prestigious college and needed to discuss it immediately, asking me to go to his property that afternoon. When I arrived, he told me that his son had been bullied and tormented by other students for not taking part in 'sexual' games among the boys. My jaw hit the floor. He wanted the names of the boys involved, their fathers' names, and for me to arrange "meetings" with them. If I had done so I would have been serving life for being an accomplice to murder. Instead, I suggested it's better to use another tactic and asked if I could speak with his son directly in order to gauge the situation and get information on the boy's fathers so we can instil anti-surveillance to mitigate and disturb any counterattack before it began. "Yes", was his simple answer as he stormed out screaming something in Arabic.

I sat with the son and was shocked by what I heard. The lads at the college were playing "sexual games with each other, but only through the most brutal of peer pressure" and manipulation from older/other students. Bullies! I fucking hate bullies. The son was a nice boy from a good family and far from who I was or my situation at that age, but I saw myself in him and my heart broke for him. The older students would film and then ransom the videos or pictures for favours, money or simply to manipulate. Essentially, blackmailing them and their families for profit but more likely a premeditated power move.

I never really got emotionally involved but this young man was clearly concerned, so I asked. Had you been involved or at very least in one of the videos "inactive". He said yes and started to cry. I feared this was the case and the true cause of his father's rage. A man normally super composed and dignified was ranting and raving. I looked the son in the eye and gave him my word I would handle this quietly and make sure that no one fucked with him again, but also not to talk to anyone else about this. I spoke to his father and told him I knew everything and would handle it. He said nothing, he walked out of the room, only to message me 'thanks' several hours later.

My unprofessional head wanted to go and beat the little bastards until they stopped moving... who were these people? Anyway, they would heal and be considered a victim; so, I went with option B. I soon had all the details we needed and invite all of the fathers to a meeting the following day. The email had full details of the information I had, and I made sure to make it clear who else was in the email. Funny old thing... these four so called VVIP's arrived from three different countries at the time and location I had dictated, on time, guilty much? Only one had security with them, who I knew and had messaged ahead of the email as a professional courtesy. He was just as shocked but agreed to remain neutral. I treated all of them with the upmost respect and apologised profusely for the manner in which I was forced to conduct my business. But! I explained if all of them were not in agreement with having their sons bring me their phones, deleting all iCloud data, and a couple of other things (I can't/won't say, as I know operators still use this tactic in the field and it may cause them unnecessary concern or issues) I needed. They all agreed and were all (great at acting) as genuinely disgusted as us. However, I understood that at least three of the fathers were central to this and just like global politics, the upper echelons of Corporate and anything else to do with power, money, or status; they had planned to blackmail my client with this footage. When three of the four arrived without security, I knew it was a rookie move and an attempt to elude me to the fact they were alone. Well, this level of security isn't a game of chess or checkers. It's a Rubik's cube of constantly evolving chess games being played in every square by the most powerful and capable narcissists you'll ever meet. Nevertheless, I had new friends now and limitless funds at my disposal, so my surveillance team were set up 48 hours prior to our meeting and monitored their teams as they moved into position over a period of four hours before the meeting, a pathetic show. My team were actually mad at the level of competence they faced. My team then mitigated their recording capabilities and sent me photos of them in their locations and the kit they'd stollen from the incompetent men now arguing where their kit had disappeared to and whose fault it was.

I shared these with the already vibrating gentleman before me, who instantly began yapping threats until I used my outdoors voice and semi-professionally warned them that I would go on the offensive if they continued; to which one replied "well, what do you call this?". I simply laughed, stepped right in his face, and told him he could always tell me to go fuck myself and we could escalate the situation, involving the law, or worse, if need be. The boys were above age consent, but I dropped in something about prison time as a paedophile for effect. Everyone calmed down and after a short more relaxed conversation where I explained that they had been the attackers and all we wanted was the issues surrounding my client solved. People I knew, knew these guys were being looked at by authorities so we were being very careful not to create ripples, let alone waves, using the cover of safeguarding my client's reputation over revenge.

The next day I was delivered all the items by my team. I sent a legendary lady who I had learnt so much from to collect the items and data, as kidnap and violence was a serious concern and females mitigate this issue nicely, especially pros; and before you start thinking I sent the girls to the slaughter, these "girls" would smash most men in a one and one fight but are far too talented for it to even come to that. True alphas that taught me so much about surveillance and professionalism I could write another book just about what they taught me. Plus, the men in question would never be linked to any form of harm to a female, with backup. The situation was over for us, although Jeffrey Epstein and friends are the perfect example that this shit is engrained in most societies.

I jumped straight back on an international tasking, feeling safer moving in the usual shadows than taking time off. This would prove a bad move, but I would find this out soon enough. Thinking I am superhuman and trying to work every hour under the sun, addicted to my craft and the opportunities coming from them. I worked standard 18-hour days and had done for years. If I was awake, I was working. I had nothing for me really, I was always on duty. All my relationships are professional, necessary. It showed, my friends and family became distant as I never attended weddings, christenings, or birthdays. I was never in one place and often couldn't tell them where I was or answer their calls. I was a ghost, lost in all the madness of the world and loving it so much I hated it.

I could feel a physical change as I pushed myself to my limits across five countries, driving endless hours and spending days pissing in bottles or hiding in plain sight. I was on a task alone as one of the team who was due to replace my colleague who had left the day before was pulled onto another location in preparation for an operation, we had been planning during my time in the country. I was awake for nearly two days monitoring cameras, changing batteries, and even conducting a solo tagging of a vehicle (never advised, always take "back watch"). I was in an apartment monitoring the cameras when I fell asleep, the motion alarms would wake me if something happened. I woke up a short time later and after a couple of seconds getting my head together, I realised I could barely open my eyes, I thought I had gone blind. I panicked and, in my hysteria, thought maybe I had been poisoned. I was on my knees and found the medical bag before again acting erratically and began injecting saline solution into my stomach, directly into my bloodstream as there was no way I could find a vein and run an IR. While doing this I decided I needed some time off. I soon calmed myself down and laid on the bed and slept for an hour or so. I woke up and could see but my face hurt, I ran to the bathroom mirror and saw that I had two huge scabby growths on the corner of each eye. It looked like I had taken a harsh beating. I sent images to my support team, and they instantly replied telling me I was to extract them, leaving all the items in the drop box and a replacement team would pick up where I left off. I was fucked. Burnt out and in need of some time off and a beer. I stepped out of this world and went on holiday with my boys. I had fun but I was exhausted, so a few wild nights and I was dead.

I had built a subtle reputation around the fact I could infiltrate areas, groups, and individuals' overtly. I'm not bragging, there are literally thousands of people better than me at surveillance, but in this area, I became a short-term anomaly. My fearless inexperience working to my favour. Surveillance companies began outsourcing specific taskings to me, with the option to utilise my own people and tactics.

Things became wild and I was constantly working to one degree or another. I couldn't turn down an opportunity or challenge. However, I had collapsed twice recently and on one occasion it had been on task. Fortunately, I was not on coverage and alone at the time, but coming around to a group of strangers around you wasn't fun. I gave myself the weekend off and booked a beautiful Sussex utopian spa weekend with a wonderful Mixed-race goddess called Mia. I had been seeing for a while; we were "on and off" as I was never around, but she was a super cool person and we got on like a house on fire. It was pure heaven! We went to dinner the night before in our robes and drank champagne until we could drink no more before returning to our room that the staff had romanticised for us. Eventually falling asleep as I almost forgot my life's little stresses for a second or two.

Reality called just after 5am the following morning in the form of a surveillance legend called Mike. I answered and he simply said, "fancy Maldives for a few days on us?". "Yep!" was my instant reply, still half pissed from the night before. Mia groaned as she rolled off me and I kissed her shoulder before sitting up in bed. "What's going on in the Maldives", I asked. Mia turned to face me throwing me a cheeky look, intensely trying to listen now. She didn't know I was into surveillance, only security. No one really knew what I did anyway. Most of their focus was on the celebs. Suited me.

Mike continued, "He's off with the non-misses for a holiday and needs you to take a picture of them together, that's it... Get it done and you're done". I said "OK". He continued with some details and my phone began vibrating with supporting emailed secure links. He asked if I was good to go and to let him know who I was taking asap. I said I was in without even looking at the emails and said, "Let me see if I can find a girl to take to the Maldives with me and I will call you back". Mia's head snapping up to look at me so fast it made me laugh. "Well, when we going baby?", she was laughing, arguably still more drunk than I was. I asked her if she fancied going to Maldives as I opened the emails and saw that the flights were in just over seven hours. She thought I was joking at first but then I started asking questions about her work and details to order a taxi to bring her passport and suggested she get her house mate to put a bag of clothes together via facetime as we didn't have time for her to spend all day doing it. Invasions had been planned in shorter time periods than Mia could arrange an outfit. She asked if I was serious, and I told her

I was. I went through the emails, and she slid under the covers to thank me.

I thought what an adventure and she thought what a touch! Free holiday. I ordered breakfast and went to work out and had a steam to sober up before driving to Mia's and then the airport. I hadn't told her we were flying first class and told her to tell the staff I had just proposed, and her ring was getting resized. Building my cover. We arrived the 36 hours prior to our target and settled in by getting to know every hotel staff team member we passed. Working our way into the fabric of our heavenly surroundings. My gorgeous guest thought I was there for a meeting and that's what I played with; Mia never asked what she assumed and then I just went with it. Staying very close to the truth is always best.

Armed with a 'company card' in hand, we set about living the dream. It was a very exclusive resort with twelve villas and a large central bar, restaurant, spa, and everything you could want. Once we arrived, I knew why I had been requested; we would have to hide in plain sight and so I set about making friends. It was the easiest job I ever had in my life as Mia and I had arrived a day before the target and set about making friends with all the staff, so we appeared a part of the furniture before he arrived. The guy turned up the morning after expected so by this time we knew everyone in the hotel, and everyone knew us. Mia was charismatic and a rare female who seemed to get on with all other females, no matter their background or beauty. Despite being stunning she had been forced to develop resilience and a robust personality as she had a background far rougher than mine; she was witty and charming and had the residents of the hotel mesmerised, leaving me to enjoy the scenery and wait for the fly to step into her web.

The first time I saw the target was in close quarters as he was checking in and we had just got back from a secluded beach, oiled up and very much looking like loves young dream enjoying paradise. I nodded to him and smiled; he returned the gesture.

I took Mia shopping, and we bought new clothes as we had both packed a little under the level required. Tonight, we needed to shine. She dragged me around for ages until she found something that made her look so incredible, she could barely keep it on around me, so much so we christened the dress even before buying it in the private changing room, we had champagne and a sofa, I mean what do you expect. We went back to get ready for the night's theatrics. I had requested we sit next to the target through my new headwaiter friend, tipping heavily to keep it our little secret. I made up that Mia really liked the girl the target was with and wanted to be her friend. He bought it or didn't give a shit. I was sat on the sofa in our lounge area when Mia walked out in something she "bought for me" on our little trip. We were nearly late for dinner as we got caught up in the moment. I was either completely in the zone or completely out of it for the first time. But I also felt happy for the first time too and was all over my duties so just went with it despite being on a task worth billions of pounds.

We arrived at dinner and heads turned as we were the youngest in the room and dressed to the nines, known to all the staff who worked a treat. We began drinking and flirting outrageously as things began to fall into place. The target arrived as our appetisers did and the girls instantly struck up a conversation. First the targets guest commented on our food, with Mia commenting on her dress. Us gents sharing a nod and awkward smile, as men do in these situations.

By the time our main course arrived I knew I had achieved stage one of the plan and managed to get within close proximity without unnerving the target. We had a genuine backstory, so I was totally relaxed as the girls spoke as I finished my desert. The live music soon started, and the girls couldn't hear one another so asked if we could join tables, we did and not long after we got several group photos. The guy barely even flinched, even smiling after encouragement from his date. The geographical location cemented the images bio data to prove time and location beyond doubt. When the job was done, he would lose a portion of his estimated 3.2-3.4 Billion in the divorce settlement because of this photo, but not before putting our dinner and the nights drinks on his room at the end of the evening as he looked to promote his status as the alpha. Either way, the job was done. I popped back to my room with Mia's phone. Pretending to grab hers instead of mine by mistake as hers had the photos on it. I sent all the details to Mike along with a back brief of my past 72 hours and requested I was given another 24 hours before they began contacting me again to tie up any loose knots and finalise the job. Basically, that meant getting out clean and not undoing the great work we've done.

It it's funny but I felt guilty the following day as despite having a genuine distaste for anyone who cheats whether male or female but felt bad that this man was going to lose nearly half of everything, he'd ever worked for made me feel bad. However, by this time I had spent an immense amount of time immersed in a world many genuinely don't even believe exists or can't comprehend because it's just so unrelatable if not unbelievable to them. I understood this well as the deeper I went into this world and the more time I spent in it the more I became alienated from the commonalities of regular people, feeling like I was the first kid to learn Santa wasn't real or just having nothing in common with pretty much anyone and everyone I knew anymore other than the people that I worked with. I knew this was an issue and I had to make a choice of Eva committing fully to this life I had chosen will deciding to step out before I came just like every other operative, I knew, dedicated to the job and the job only as it was all they had. Ironically, it was spending this time with Mia that made me realise I wanted more. My mother was also deteriorating mentally, and I wanted to spend as much time with her as I could before I lost my idol and the mother I knew and had all but decided by the time we landed back in London Gatwick airport that it was time for me to once again mix things up and look for other opportunities.

I didn't know it, but I should have stayed doing what I was. My next job would be the most stressful and dangerous I would ever take on. My only regret is professional regret, to this day.

Chapter 9
FILM & TV

I landed at London Heathrow after a short yet sweet job in Dubai. I switched my phone on and it exploded with messages and emails as per usual. It had become a personal joke of mine. "Here we go", flights had become my only me time.

I started perusing the messages as they continued to come through, my phone rang and it was a surveillance friend of mine who didn't bother with pleasantries, instead simply asking, "back and available? He then asked if I was available for a fast ball, leaving London, Heathrow in four hours. I was still on the runway from my last job but listen as he told me I would be going to South Africa for several days protecting the corporate representative of a film studio. I told him I was already at Heathrow but would go home and switch my bags and kit before returning to the airport with plenty of time.

I have great friends and contacts in South Africa since attending the Ronin Close Protection course there. Considered the best bodyguarding and high-risk paramedic course in the world, as I mentioned earlier. I

217

was very happy to finish as Top Student and be welcomed into the amazing network and gain the support of Timm Smith, the creator of Ronin, and long-time bodyguard to Mr Nelson Mandela. I learnt from the best.

So! After a quick cup of coffee with my mum and exchanging kit and clothes with the shed, that was now pretty much just a storage room for my clothes and kit, rather than bedroom; I was back in a taxi and on my way to Heathrow. Messaging with friends and colleagues from SA whilst on route to the airport to let them know I would soon be in the country, a professional courtesy at the very least.

Fighting my way through the holiday crowds, I eventually made it to the Virgin lounge where I was due to meet my principle. The Virgin Airways lounge was fantastic! I walked into the lounge and a lady's head spun and caught my attention; she waved and as I walked over, she blushed and smiled. As I sat down, she introduced herself, I went to do the same and she cut me off asking how old I was, only to continue talking over me, "you are far too handsome to be bloody bodyguard. How old are you?". This pissed me off immensely, but I career laughed and simply said "thank you, I am 32". I switched up the conversation by telling her I had contacted my people in the country, who were on standby should we need. She got the message and took my lead, briefing me on the situation.

A crew member had been shot, he was local, doing ok, and would fully recover; our role was to investigate from a corporate position whilst supporting local police and ensure everything was being done to protect the crew, and investment (the production/film). After an awkward beginning, things settled and we began talking about this and that in relation to her position, turned out we knew a lot of same people and quickly began to get along.

I felt a little uncomfortable as she had looked at me like lunch, making subtle inappropriate comments that had unfortunately become a regular thing whenever working with female superiors older than myself; it had simply become a reality of the job, as bad as that sounds. Sexual harassment and abuse are only acknowledged one way and would damage my reputation should I complain, and it had honestly become so normal I didn't really care unless it undermined my skills and professionalism, so I stayed quiet. Things got a little more awkward as we boarded the flight and took our seats that were a couple of seats away from each other, yet facing inwards so we almost faced each other. We continued talking and she told me I could relax, eat, and drink what I liked. As she did, the stewardess came over, and I shit you not, instead of asking me what size pyjamas I would like, she asked me, "what will you be wearing tonight?" before laughing out loud at herself, owning the situation, and very politely and excessively apologising to me as we laughed with the rest of the cabin who had heard; it created a great cabin atmosphere to be fair. Virgin First Class was awesome, the best in fact. I would normally be protecting someone very famous or someone with a high threat level, so couldn't relax to a degree. This time was completely different. I took full advantage and allowed myself a glass of champagne before take-off as I took in the crystal décor and stunning

Virgin staff and their wonderful service. I remember thinking, I could get used to this! I settled and realised in that moment I needed to level up, my professional head not allowing me to see the enjoyment in such blessing previously, as I was laser focussed and engrossed in my duties. I relaxed for the first time in months, enjoyed another glass of champagne and settled into my favourite place, 34,000 ft in the sky, with no signal.

We arrived in South Africa and the first thing the corporate representative (let's call her Susie) said was, "I hope you gave her your number?". I just laughed, because I had; meeting up with her and her friends in Johannesburg a couple of months later.

Gift, our awesome driver collected us. We quickly became friends as I bombarded him with questions about culture and local politics. Gift is one of those people you meet and instantly love; a gentle giant who is always fussing over others whilst dedicating himself to his family, duties and dreams. We are friends to this day.

The production was filming in the Eastern Cape. It's a beautiful part of the world, and the perfect place to shoot a remake of The Jungle Book with a wonderfully talented cast, director, and crew. I had been on film sets many times before with clients but hadn't had the opportunity to freely wander around and get to meet the crew and feel part of a production. It was amazing.

As I mentioned previously, I had studied media production and communication at college, then journalism, news media and cultural studies at university; I had always wanted to get back to film, it was my dream and always had been, I just got last along away. Taking the opportunity before me to protecting the content, rather than creating it.

After a couple of days of settling in, I made friends with the lead actor Rohan and his wonderful family. I then managed to persuade the local police chief to come and set up and support us on some of the issues we were facing. Gift had told me the local police chief was a Zulu, like him. He taught me how to give the Zulu handshake of respect and how to best present myself culturally. I tried with Susie previously, but he wouldn't acknowledge her, it's a cultural thing. She was extremely intelligent and worldly seasoned and had predicted this. This time, however, armed with Gifts suggestions, he agreed to come down. I spoke to him as a human and equal rather than trying to dictate his duties to him (a pet hate of any public servant), and as I thanked him, I used the Zulu handshake Gift had shown me, and he actually giggled.

Later that day Susie asked if I would stay on for the rest of production? which would mean extending my trip from six days to around six weeks. I said of course. The job was amazing, I spent the rest of the trip supporting the production in the jungle, I went on safari, I spent a week driving the Eastern Cape in convoy; working with some true legends to capture the most beautiful sunrises and sunsets. This was it, no more daily life-threatening situations, mitigating the kidnap of client's children or stressing until my eyes bleed jobs for me, this was the future. My future. I hadn't thought about myself in a while.

After nearly seven amazing weeks in beautiful South Africa, it was time to go home. I had completely fallen in love with the country, its people, the production crew. One night I had dinner with the director Andy Serkis and his lovely assistant Catherine (now producer). Both truly wonderful people. Andy could not have been nicer and if he wasn't one of my favourite people in the industry prior to this, he soon become top of the pack. What pleasure to meet someone who treats all around them so well, and with such respect, a true honour. Truly lovely people. I was hooked! Sadly, for now, it was time to go home. After an extended stopover in Johannesburg to catch up with the charming flight attendant. After a few dangerous drinks and a backdoor escape from a bar into my private car to escape a knifeman and a debaucherous night at the best hotel in town later, I was back in Virgin First Class exhausted but feeling mentally refreshed after having some fun after literally years of nothing but intense work.

I landed back in London and wasn't even through customs when Susie called to invite me to an interview the following day; telling me I needed a break from the madness and would be a great fit for the studios "crown jewel" of a production that was suffering heavily from internal issues. I was so excited at the opportunity to relax for a while and be close to my mum, I accepted the invitation immediately and cleared my schedule. Calling my mum on the way to her house, like any good mamma's boy would. She was so happy and when I arrived at her house she came outside, and we had a little cuddle and dance. One of those moments that stays with you forever.

Warming your heart on a cold day. She was happy because I would be working in a safer environment and would be home to see her more regularly. She didn't know what operations I had been on, or even that I had been a surveillance operative; but she saw me each time I came home, exhausted and wrecked. Telling me, "I watched you learn to lie, so just be honest with me and then I know you are ok". We went out for a nice meal to talk about it, and I managed to change the subject to giving her some money before just relaxing and having fun, before getting a well-deserved early night.

I interviewed the following morning but was warned there was a lady there who did not want security or any support for that matter; she had been head of locations for many years and had an impressive resume so I didn't understand what the problem would be. If anything, I would have thought this woman would have been the one to request security and despite everything that I had been briefed, I was excited to meet her as those with reputations such as this are often the best at what they do, and others are just second hand haters.

Essentially, it would be my job to support and advise her team on security measures that would protect the magical work her team and the rest of the crew worked so hard to achieve. However, when I entered the room her attitude towards me stifled the room. This was a new one for me, but I was used to uncomfortable prickly situations and there were six others in the room I chose to focus on as I spoke. They all seemed nice enough so thought maybe she was just tired or having a bad day. However, I should have left that office and gone back to the safety of protecting my clients from armed kidnap threats, it would have been safer. I mean, in hindsight, rollie pollies through a mine field would have probably been safer too.

I left the interview and went home. I had a bad feeling so made some calls to pre-emptively let my contacts know I would likely be available as of the following day but would call back to confirm once WB had done so with me. The next morning, I received a call from Susie offering me the position as head of security for the production we discussed, Fantastic Beasts. I started Monday, but not before taking my extended family out for a meal to celebrate.

I had my first weekend off in months and this new opportunity meant I would be able to have a social life again as it was only five days a week and on paper it was so easy I wasn't sure I wanted it as I would get bored easily. Plus, I was getting back to my original dream that I had all but eradicated from my mind as just a dream. Film. The only thing I loved nearly as much as animals. Don't laugh. It is true. Animals are the best people.

I had dreamt of the beautiful artistic and creative side of film for years and always dreamt of writing and acting, but security had been all consuming. I had been writing for fun since the Marines, but my job was to protect the magic, not be a part of it. However, from the very first day I knew the dream was going to have to wait a little longer. I would not be able to gravitate into the creative world just yet as the state of security on set and at the studio in general was so bad, I found it funny. In fact, there was blatant criminality and debauchery going on; meaning this was going to be the most dangerous and dirty detail yet. And I am not exaggerating. I was completely shocked and instantly regretted my decision. This was going to be dangerous for me as the criminality was normalised and those pulling the strings sat in powerful positions with the ear of people like the prickly lady who interviewed me. So they had the trust of these people too.

Day one I met the problem and realised the magnitude of it. I walked around the studio on my first day to meet the third-party security team, locations manager, crew, and introduce myself. I was stunned at how bad site security was but especially the level of security directly supporting the production. It literally made no sense to me. There were white guys with black guys SIA Licenses (Security Industry Authority – the UK minimum standard) on one side of the set, and black guys with a white guy's SIA badge on the other. When I asked why they had someone else's SIA badge, they laughed, and one of them told me he had only got out of prison three weeks ago so couldn't get his own one. To this day I don't know if he was just that stupid or was so seasoned in this shower of shite of a security team that he deemed it normal. I continued my introduction to my wonderful new team; some were sleeping, most were watching their phones, others told me openly how shit it was working there and just moaned for the entirety of our introduction. It was genuinely funny at the time. I sent pictures to Susie and updated her verbally on my findings and she simply told me to get to work.

The lines between individuals and external companies were blurred. It was a haven for fraud and corruption. I was flabbergasted and retreated to my office and printed out all the documents and information I had in a desperate attempt to make it make sense. I spread it across my desk but before I had finished laying it out, I saw the security numbers were inflated to a ridiculous standard. Three guards on a single position normally requiring one; not to mention that there was also a large site security team supporting them. What are we protecting? the crown jewels! And where was all this security. Ghost shifts and no shows no doubt. I made some notes and with the information I had wiped nearly £200,000 off the security budget, in literally five minutes. This was unreal. Either I didn't know what I was doing, and this was like fingerpainting compared to what I had done my career, or someone was corrupt as fuck.

I went to find the location's manager and as I approached her, before I could speak, she said something that I will never forget. She told me that she had just received a call from our current security company who found out I was on set and reacted by stepping off the job; apparently no longer interested in a job paying around £50,000 per week. The fraud and criminality were so obvious I felt embarrassed to be stood there with a straight face. I had just come from working with true professionals I aspired to be like in many ways. People that inspired me every day as I learnt and grew through their examples. Meanwhile these guys are sneaking prostitutes into the crowded tent during the night shift, doing and selling drugs openly and the location manager is clearly at the centre of it. Even stealing things from production, repackaging as if from her own company and selling them back to the production. Let me remind you, this is still my first day.

This person: let's call her Hooch, either thought I was dumb, or corruptible. Well, I have been many things in my life, but my integrity and word have always been worth more to me than anything money can buy. You know my story by now and I was no boy scout. I saw it as someone owning me and having the power to manipulate me in the future so always avoided anything that would have me end up in someone's pocket and at their disposal. I mean, by this time I had taken no less than nine polygraphs and was always paid well so why would I risk all that for anything but life changing money? You wouldn't, right? Besides, it would be an instant career ender and I would know, even if no one else did.

The fact that there was barely any consideration for illusion, and the way Hooch casually incriminated herself, genuinely worried and confused me. I wanted to get out of there immediately and back to fair fights and real security work. I knew this person was the string puller. She was so fake in her attempts to be my best friend whilst talking shit about everyone on site, everyone! Producers, security, crew; even the prickly women from my interview who actually her boss and strategically adopted godmother to her daughter. Now I understood it all perfectly. Let me tell you a little secret, if anyone is always talking shit about other people, they're also talking that way about you when

227

you are not around. It's a habit, a character trait, you're not a wonderful oasis where they feel safe expressing their feelings, it's a habit, they're talking shit about you too.

Side note: Manipulation is a beta trait, remove their power by not spreading the bullshit.

I instantly regretted taking the job, I went back to my office and sat there for the longest time deciding whether to walk out and go back to my adventures. Eventually deciding I would humbly request to be replaced as it was only my first day and the best time for some other poor bastard to step in. However, life is a funny thing as I walked down to set, I bumped into a guy I used to work with. I knew him well so I could speak openly and told him what was going on; without flinching, he said, "oh you've met her then have you?". He began telling me pretty much everything I needed to know about her links to the criminal world, her on-site and on-set activities and her documented character assassination attempts of everyone whilst pretending to be their friends. By the end of our conversation, for one stupid reason or another, I had decided to stay and give it a go. My mum was happy and maybe I would just stay long enough to get rid of this person before going back to playing 007. A goodwill gesture to an industry I longed to be a part of, or so I thought.

Now before it sounds like I am shiting on the film industry. Please understand that I love the film industry. There is nothing like it and there are such a wonderful bunch of creative, positive, open-minded people that have worked on each-and-every production I've had the honour of working with. However, I was forced to deal with the supportive personnel and tribal culture built upon nepotism and the ability to easily defraud productions who weren't paying attention or just accepted it as to speak out was to be fired. My job was to protect the magic, not be a part of it as I have said.

It transpired; the location manager was *allegedly* receiving £1 per security person, per hour. Answering a lot of questions. I generally didn't care about this level of fraud as this goes on at every level in the world. However, the issue was the shit standard of the security guard that was being supplied, costing us as a production £15 per person per hour. The guard themselves being paid around £9. So, we were getting a £9 standard guard for the price of £15. Plus, some companies relieved their guards of the travel/millage allowance money we gave them and portions of their meal allowance. Despite them being fed with the rest of the crew twice a day. So, our guards working with us weren't getting any of the benefits and therefore not receiving the incentives to focus and become a part of a team and do their fucking job. Well, this was about to stop. I would be attacked, character assassinated, and bullied like no other time in my life. Good! Bring it on... I fucking hate bullies!

I soon began hearing rumours about myself. Apparently, I was due to conduct background checks on everyone in production and was actively trying to hack everyone's social media. More laughable bullshit to baffle brains. But with a security team more criminal and twice as stupid as the boy I once was, it did the job to create the desired divide.

I was unaware of any of this undercurrent of bullshit until asked directly by an Assistant Director (AD) whom I had been working closely with. I thanked him for asking questions, and reassured him with facts, that it was nonsense. Explaining as I proved my points to him using easily accessed websites, noting specifically that background checks required the person it is on to provide consent and how serious a crime of hacking into accounts is, asking him if he thought we had the budget? The time? and what would the production get from it? He got it right away. Helping to spread facts, not fiction. I even posted step-by-step procedures that noted our full scope of security procedures. Legal background checks cost a couple of £100 and take around six weeks; to monitor 400 social medias, plus Supporting Artists. Ridiculous! I would need three of me working 24/7. In all honesty I became bitter, stuck in political battles with people I couldn't ignore as they were the issue. It blew my mind. However, I stuck to my professional guns and hired a former Royal Marine friend as my number 2 so he could do the leg work, freeing me to manage our internal issues. Attempting to create at least a small team, standardised, and supporting each other, dare I say to the benefit of the production. However, hiring this person was also a huge mistake. Handing people something they haven't earned is always going to end in disaster.

If you haven't got it yet, this was my personal hell. Toxic atmospherics and the easiest job in the world made horrendously bad because of politics and nepotism. Spoilt in such an amazing industry, the people causing the issues were always the talentless, never the dedicated, so at least this made sense to me. However, some people become a product of their environment and my number 2 soon dropped standards and even called a prostitute to his room whilst we were away on task. Coming to my house to tell me after his girlfriend found out whilst he was meant to be on set managing a busy morning for us after I let him leave early the previous day.

We concluded the production, and I was over the fucking moon. Zero leaks or major external issues, and no official incidents; but it wasn't great. I found it tremendously hard not to lose my shit on the daily and my limits were pushed when one day, one of the young AD girls came up to me and nervously told me that Steve, a doorman turned security officer we had in our extended team, would go up to some of the young girls when they were tired or stressing out and say, "hug time?", with his arms spread. I literally had to be grabbed by one of the other members of the team as I knew he was on site and wanted to beat some decency into him. I spoke with Steve and his boss separately, his boss cried in my office because I was shouting at him, pathetic crocodile tears; I very nearly lost my job and freedom that day. Diverse approaches to discipline, professionalism and a difference in opinion are one thing; being void of morals and choosing to bully for financial gain are a complete other. But then I have always been rather sensitive to bullies and anyone who thinks it's ok to mess with anyone within my realm of responsibility.

The issue for studios is much like any other major investment, brand, or corporation that has been heavily invested in and provides food on the table for hundreds, if not thousands of people. Or just a couple of wealthy, highly influential and powerful people. Therefore, the investment/interest will be protected to a degree that supersedes morality. This is life. Film is the perfect example of this, as with hundreds of millions of pounds invested, a production must be aggressively protected if it is going to survive the assault course of controversies surrounding it. Most are nothing sinister, but with the media always sensationalising or looking to leak story lines or other intellectual property, a single news article or sour crew member can cause mayhem. The media knows no grey areas because people like drama, and drama is their business. Frustratingly, this results in the studios being unable to punish or openly prosecute crew without drawing unwanted attention. Money trumps morality, I can guarantee you that. I have seen it over and over again with evil paying off the innocent, buying not just this victim's silence but subsequently setting up the next victim in the process, all in a single money exchange. A culture and system that empowers and protects people not because of their power or status, but the lack of accountability of each and every person in any given situation that didn't highlight issues in their infancy or who chose to stay quiet for job security or progression. For change to come, everyone aware would have to sacrifice their career and be easily replaced; unhindered accountability and action solve most of the world's problems, but most of the world have families and duties to others that supersede these broader issues. It doesn't make them bad people, not at all. But the bad people manipulate these situations, and the issues continue.

The film industry has been in the news the past few years for all the wrong reasons but if the media presented genuine reality of it all then the public would better understand the culture and subsequently empower the industry to bring in real change. But it takes people cemented in their positions to speak out and lose all they have. From studio security, to producers, to those who make the choice to succumb to the culture only to complain about it as they support it with their active inclusion. Some studios have instead taken the steps to hire 'HR managers' to sit in front of lawyers and stop complaints and change starting in the first place. I have emails in my account that would make you scream in disbelief that prove this. (screen shots of such emails are presented at the end of this book)

I was offered a second major production at the same studio. Despite many thinking I would not be invited back or chose to come back. I was legit and got the job done, and that's all that mattered at this point. I interviewed for the position and was told I was "too good looking for the job". I am being serious, what the actual fuck. Even though they were half joking I was incensed and when I started, I was treated like a bimbo. Being given someone with no experience or interest in their role as my number 2. She was rarely at work and if she was, she was attached to marketing as she hunted for her next role as most did.

Using security as a steppingstone. Hence the shitty state of it. She had free roam because the production UPM had been promised a producer's role by a powerful EMMY winner if she helped her. So, I was fucked and just got on with it. Enjoy busying myself looking out for the awesome cast who were a dream to work with. As were the rest of the extended crew and especially the location department who were fantastic at their job and a dream to work with, especially after my first experience.

I was miserable, my girlfriend and I had a huge argument one morning because my phone number was across the studio for anyone to with security issues or questions for our production to call. I would often get messages, pictures and videos from girls working on the production being cheeky and trying their luck, but this one morning my girlfriend saw a list of names in my WhatsApp and asked to see, I let her as I hadn't tried to hide them and hadn't messaged back. She lost her shit and left, flying back to the US. I understood, I was gutted but didn't show it, and understood how she felt. I should have gone with her. I was never around; I was now working 130 hours a week and completely miserable when not working. My mother wasn't doing so well and so wanted to spend the time I had with her. I decided I would do one more production, only after I had some fun!

I called Adam who was on a yacht in the Mediterranean, now an engineer. Within hours we had booked a three-month trip. Indonesia – Vietnam – Laos, and Thailand. It was time to enjoy the fruits of my labour for once. This allowed me to get through the next few months. In fact, I started to enjoy it as I started looking after the cast more than I did the film that had become so difficult due to the fact the crew were almost rebelling at their treatment. Even the Director was under attack. Eventually they fired him not long after his daughter committed suicide. Wonderful people. I formed a professional relationship with Ben Affleck who is a genuine and awesome person and after his assistant emailed the studio to tell them I was the best security he had ever had, things got easier for me. I cruised after this, giving zero fucks what anyone thought as this let me know I was doing the right thing and I would soon be on a flight to paradise with Adam.

Before we even got on the plane, I felt a little like me again. Bali was the first stop, and we had a great time bouncing around the islands and living the Bali dream. It felt amazing to shed my usual materialistic atmospherics and have genuine conversations with grateful and happy locals. One night Adam and I met some local lads sharing a beer and playing the guitar, all singing songs they knew. We asked to join and bought all the beer from the local store as a thank you. The small gathering turned into a mini party with them welcoming us into their world, where people are valued over everything else. It was an incredible night where Adamski got lost and ended up in a horse stable. I made it home wearing a towel as I exited the jungle to my room door.

Next it was Vietnam, I fell in love with Sapa. North Mongol tribes people walking us ancient routes to homestays where families fed us and pointed us to a tiny local bar! Amazing times. We landed in Laos and got two scooters and hit the road, riding 5-hours Viengko. It's a hippy town in the mountains with a river that runs for miles, and has bars and restaurants sporadically dotted along the route, where the locals throw ropes and use sticks to pull you in. The last thing I remember I was going down a zip line with three girls hanging onto me, all blind drunk, the local rum too much for me, especially as I had been made to down a pint of it at each stop as Adamski proudly dropped me in it, telling everyone it was my birthday, which it was. I was 33 and living the dream. In the middle of nowhere with my best pal, away from all the drama and letting loose. I woke up in my bed, Adam thrusting food in my face and excitingly telling me he had the best birthday present for me. Eating my noodles in the shower, yes in the shower, Adam told me he got us tickets to a jungle party. The girls from the zip line had invited us. We were picked up outside a bar and driven in took-took through the jungle on roads that weren't there until the music was built and built and the fires and lights came into view through the trees. Oh, it was on.

We walked into one of the parties I've ever been to. We jumped out the back of the took-took and our group headed straight for the dance floor that had a huge bonfire in the middle of it and there were people from all over the world having an awesome time. We went to the bar and the first thing we were offered was a mushroom shake. After we stopped laughing and daring each other to do it we both said fuck it and ordered one each. The lady said we should share one but that isn't the way we do things, it's always all or nothing. The shakes were nice, and we quickly downed them before ordering some beers and heading back to the dance floor where we told the girls what we had just done whilst giggling like little schoolboys. I have been dancing and joking around for about half an hour before people's faces start to turn into bright blue skulls. I had definitely bitten off more than I can chew but when I looked to Adam who was clearly in his own world, laughing at himself. We caught each other's eye and again started laughing like little naughty schoolboys. The night escalated from there and we wandered around the awesome location in the jungle with huge bonfires dotted everywhere. Dancing and meeting people from all over the world, it was incredible.

We sat around a bonfire just on the edge of the jungle and got out a large bag of weed. There with people from fourteen different countries, sat in the jungle, I had no idea where I was, but it felt like heaven. For the first time in the longest time, I felt free and inspired. Such beautiful souls just enjoying each other's company and the experience. Nothing but love. I have never been one to advocate for drugs but this night they really helped me break some personal barriers and look at the bigger picture. Recognising the deterioration of my mental health since joining the industry and the things I really wanted to do in life. With my mental constraints removed, I was free to think outside the box and be truly honest with myself.

Removing the limitations, I put myself in dedication to the opportunities I had been privileged to be offered made me realise just how miserable I had become. You can go a long way down the wrong road and end up further away from where you wanted than when you started if you don't pay attention. But for now, it was time to enjoy the party. What a night! Eventually it came to an end and as we entered the took-took back to reality.

We chilled out the next day and said goodbye to all our friends before heading to our destination. Thailand. Chiang Mai, elephant sanctuaries, Muay Thai, the best food on earth, where the people are genuinely kind and can party with the best of them. A wonderful place and culture.

Whilst away I was asked to do Fantastic Beasts 2, I wanted it like a bullet to the brain but needed a little more time to materialise something else I was working towards. So, I said yes, but I had to be in control of the security budget. Hooch had been removed from any future productions after my investigations and pressure unveiled her criminal ways, and everything ran smoothly. The problem had been removed. Oh, apart from her friend's security company who stepped in on FB1 as 'replacement' of the company who walked off on the first film, when they almost went bust and ended up in an internal legal dispute. A very good company where one silly man nearly ruined it for the others as he was so confident the man, they called Mr "Shitty" (Hooches replacement) had his back. Hooch's replacement wasn't as well versed, and I was forced to bring in another company. A great one that supported us for the rest of the production without any issues other than the guys I kept on from the previous company out of misplaced loyalty. But that was enough for me... I got out of there. I started consulting here and there whilst managing my usual bits and pieces, but I wanted something new; in fact, I needed it!

I then went to visit my mum who had since retired to Spain for some lovely mother and son time. After a week or so I sat with my mum in Spain nursing a heavy hangover and my mother laughing at me as my phone rang, and I jumped. I answered and was asked to interview as a candidate for Close Protection for F. Gary Grey who was being hunted by the infamous Suge Knight, a gang member and CEO of Death Row records. I knew all the players and grew up listening to Dr. Dre and Snoop and that genre so was excited to be a very small part of this world. This is all public record, but Suge killed a man whilst attempting to get to Gary on the film set of the incredible NWA film. Gary was naturally concerned and wanted to be able to focus on his new film, so the production put the wheels in motion. I flew back to London and interviewed; they were very cool people, and I knew I had the job as I fit the required dynamic and requirements perfectly. The client liked me as he liked his privacy.

The following day I received a call from the head of Sony security saying I had secured the position, and could I be available the following week for recce to Italy? I said of course.

The plan was to work together and essentially see if we got along before confirming the contract for the entirety of the film. Believe me when I say that the relationship between protector and principal is vital in order to put in place mitigations and fulfil their obligations to the fullest.

I think it is fair to say that we got along like a house on fire whilst we were in Italy, and he told me he was going to tell the studio I was the man he wanted. I liked Gary a lot. A proper man's man who expected me to do my job and then left me to it. During my audition he had spoken about someone who had infiltrated his security team and he gave me some information name details and showed me a picture. I told him I would investigate and made a call. I returned to him five minutes later and told him that he had shown me the wrong picture. It wasn't in line with the other details. I showed him the correct picture and he laughed out loud. "That's the guy" he said to Charlie, his Executive Assistant, and an independent director in his own right.

We landed back in London, and I was told I would start the full-time position the following Tuesday; it was now Saturday morning. This caused a bit of an issue for me but didn't let on. I raced home, booked what I needed to book, packed what I needed to pack and put my beautiful French Bulldogs Lilo and Stitch into the car before driving the 21-hour journey to my mum's villa where the dogs would stay until the end of my detail. I know this will sound crazy to a lot of people out there and maybe not so crazy to others but realising that I would not see my dogs for many months was heart breaking. I adore my dogs; I adore animals in general. I have always preferred animals to people, my career cemented this. I didn't stop and drove directly so I would be able to have a whole day with them in Spain before returning to start my role as the director's bodyguard and head of production security for Men In Black International.

We shot the film in the UK, Morocco, and Italy with the genuinely awesome Chris Hemsworth and Tessa Thompson. They are two of my favourite celebs I have ever met and all of the people around them were equally as lovely. Refreshing!

I had a lot on my plate during this production as you can imagine. I had a web of others provide me with all the intel I needed but this only reassured my actions as Suge Knight looked to find Gary and hurt or humiliate him in an attempt to show the world he was still powerful. But this was my world, not his.

Several individuals, groups, and gangs looked to gain clout on both sides of the pond but attempting to do Suges bidding or gain favours, so I had to work around the clock to stay one step ahead until the web was set up. These people weren't even playing checkers, let alone chess, but they only had to get lucky once. Eventually I got tired of this and went on the attack. Sending some of these people their locations with a message. They were well out of their depth and after the two individuals we had eyes on flew to the UK, everyone knew it.

I met the two gentlemen who had flown over from LA London Heathrow whilst holding a name card. Posing as their driver with two of my boys from Walthamstow stood back by the WH Smiths store so they could see them but would not gain too much attention. I welcomed the two travellers before very calmly and respectfully explaining to them that London was my town and if they stepped outside the airport, it would be extremely unlikely they'd be able to walk back in. I did offer an out and suggested they go somewhere else, adding, they could tell their people whatever story they wanted to and save face, I wouldn't be mentioning this situation to anyone. I was not from the street, but I could take it there without any issues nodding over to my friends. They told me to go fuck myself, but their words did not hide their eyes and I knew there would not be any issue so excused myself and spoke to my friends before I left for the studio; leaving the fine gentlemen in the capable hands of my friends who informed me five or six hours later that the gentleman had decided to fly on to Paris. Good move gents.

I was having fun again and enjoying security, but I had decided this would be my last job for a while. I desperately needed a break, so after the film concluded I went to Rome for a bit of R&R. Chased beautiful women and ate all the beautiful foods. I then flew to Valencia to pick up Lilo & Stitch before moving to Barcelona. Only leaving for the MiBI and Spiderman press tours in Beijing and the UK. Providing coverage for F Gary Grey and the home-grown legend that is Tom Holland. Now Tom is a very good-looking boy and I'm not trying to take anything away from him at all, but I thought Chris Hemsworth was one of the most attractive and popular men on the planet. However, when we got to Beijing, I could not believe how crazy the girls were going for Tom compared to how they had done so Chris. It was insane and at times I literally had girls on each shoulder, gently moving them from blocking our exit. Again, Tom, his brother Harry and his family were truly wonderful people. I felt now was a good time to take a break. Ending it on a high note.

I moved back to beautiful Barcelona and took my life by the horns and took the UCLA script writing course. I was finally getting the courage to revisit my childhood passion of film production and writing but this time I was going to be the content, the creator, I wouldn't let anything, or anyone get in my way... or so I thought!

JT, my Royal Marine brother did something I never expected and pulled the rug from underneath me, getting drunk whilst on duty and losing me a huge contract I had worked three years for that would support my new venture. Giving me the freedom to pursue my dream. I realised I couldn't leave the business without constant super vision and in this moment, I began to lose faith in my ability to get out; I began to lose the spark that brought me success and became bitter at being used by everyone, especially those I had helped most. From a factory in Birmingham to second in charge of a major production – but people are who they are because of who they are – anything given will be lost and nothing gained without them conquering themselves first, through suffering, wasted. Like a pig in a Tom Ford suit. But I had yet to accept this included my nearest and dearest. Over the next few months, I would begin to lose three very important relationships that in hindsight began my mental health spiral, and for the first time in years sent me down a very bitter road.

I had to go back to work, and this pissed me off. I had rented a wonderful beach apartment and was chilling out with Lilo and Stitch every day. Taking time away from humans whilst considering what I really wanted in life. It is here I should have stayed. I knew I hated the corporate industry and needed some love and humanity in my life. Heavy lies the crown and the responsibility I had for such a prolonged period had alienated me from most people I knew as they saw my intensity as scary or intimidating rather than someone who was intensely busy managing the safety of others. I decided to turn off my phone and go wild. I should have stayed focussed and taken one of the opportunities I had been offered to act, but I couldn't step out of the shadows just yet and I knew it.

At this point I was dating an A list celebrity in secret but one night we were caught out together by the paparazzi whilst having dinner at Bluebird, in Chelsea, London. We had managed to keep it a secret from everyone for months despite her getting upset when I went from holding her hand to stepping back and pretending to be her bodyguard whenever out in public. A consideration to protect her and not dissolve her concern I was with her for fame. As we left Bluebird and clearly together a flash from a pap's camera brought me back to reality and I reverted to my bodyguarding position and put her into the car before jumping in the front. I spoke to the pap I knew very well and asked him to delete the picture as it looked unprofessional for me, and I was consoling her. He said bullshit but wanted the exclusive when we came out officially, I agreed. When I got into the car she was cry and when we arrived back at her house, we had a huge argument where she wanted us to be official. This would better suit her than me as I would have to step away from my company and career and tr to become what exactly? We calmed down and she suggested she have her publicist come over to discuss. I thought she meant the following day but instead she arrived within the hour, and we sat up all night discussing how things would go. The sun rose and I left after a heart-breaking goodbye, I couldn't throw away my career and I couldn't watch her suffer anymore. Now I was just miserable. I went back to Barcelona and ignored the world for months.

After a couple of months of feeling sorry for myself and trying to decide what to do, I received a call from Netflix. Asking if I would meet the new head of Security for EMEA to discuss an opportunity. I did, another bad mistake but one based on false sales and promises by another former Marine. I should have stayed away as it was the same corporate nonsense and corruption. I moved back to the UK and picked up all the bad habits, rituals, and processes I had worked so hard to overcome. Surrounded with negatives they came back with a vengeance! I was drowning in the bullshit of the choices I had made and as we entered 2020, I was living back in the UK doing a job nothing like the one promised, in a country I that no longer felt at home, and as news of my friends dropping like flies came in thick and fast as suicide began to ravage my brothers from across the world as the Covid saga changed everything for ever.

The pain and helplessness I felt at losing people I cherished and admired really hurt me and the pain began to fuel a bitterness for the life I was living and desperation for an escape plan. I needed to feel again. I needed purpose. I had lots of people to do things with but no one to do my nothings with, my work had become a burden, not a blessing. I decided it was dream hunting time. This time I was going to go all in.

Chapter 10
THE FLOOD GATES

I had been immersed in a world of excellence ever since escaping to the Royal Marines; filled with purpose and a dream for better, to be better. However, something had changed in me since leaving the realm of excellence and beginning my civilian journey. I missed the virtuousness, the comradery, the genuine pursuit of excellence and challenge that had given me the purpose and self-value I had craved so deeply, even if I didn't know it. The adventures I had been on, and the level of intensity was much more addictive, but I never really looked up. I never smelt the flowers; I didn't enjoy those moments as I could have. I just steamed onto the next challenge. Loving every minute of it as I felt the distance and difference between the person I was when I started this crazy life, and the person who I had become. However, I was so engrossed and disciplined that there was never time or benefit to reflect or enjoy anything as it was always onto the next thing with professional lessons learnt.

Growth was the result, ambition the vessel, and my fear of a life of silent desperation, the fuel. I had the honour of operating with and working for the world's elite. Every single one of them inspirational in their pursuit of excellence; achieving and then maintaining their excellence by continuously revaluating their approach and evolving in real time to remain flexible and adaptable to any opportunity that might arise. Working endlessly to compete with who they were yesterday, not who someone else is today. Using other people's success as inspiration to drive them. The culture was you against you, and that we all go through this life alone together. No one owes you anything. But once you achieve a standard and mindset it bonds you to people with the same mindset as you exude the ethos because you live the ethos, therefore you attract it. Excellence has a humble, yet confident swagger earned with the acceptance that the more you learn, the less you know. That you are a mortal that makes mistakes, gets tired, hungry, lazy, and sad; you will always be different because you are unique, you are you, and that is your superpower. Those who embrace their inner weirdo and dedicate themselves to honest reflection, adaption, and action always win, eventually. No limits.

I have met so many legends I can promise you what you think is impossible has likely already been done. You are thinking too small. Then again, I have been extremely fortunate to have been inspired by genuine heroes and legends around the globe. Finding myself in all kinds of serial and often dangerous places. To name a few: I operated with a female medic in her 20's who was attached to us in Helmand Province, Afghanistan; I have met Zulu tribesmen that became Hollywood film crew, female

Apache helicopter pilots, a modern-day slave who escaped Africa to become a chauffeur for celebrities on UK productions; and a scroll of other legends I was fortunate to meet. The world is full of incredible people and incredible experiences. I missed the elite culture of unity and having the opportunity to take inspiration from everyone and everything I was immersed in. Too focussed and tight at times, I guess. But not all games are compulsory for everyone, and these are often the game's most dream of playing. I had stepped away from the wolfpack and was now hanging with sheep. The desire to be a sheepdog was fading away as I became lost and frustrate with the normality of ignorance that surrounded me. Except, whilst writing this book I have gained an immense amount of gratitude for my life. Who gets to do what I did? I mean I would like to take all the credit but the places I ended up through luck has been incredible. I just always said yes. Fuck it, why not? was how I looked at life as I always planned for tomorrow with the acceptance it could always be my final day.

At this point I had given up trying to fit in, the only time in my life I had really tried. I had dedicated myself to being a sheepdog, protecting the sheep from the wolves who had tried to recruit me all my life. Risking my life and seeing the lives of those doing the same suffering immensely, as mothers missed their children's first steps, fathers missed the birth of their first born, and dear john letters flooded in like Chris Hemsworth post on Valentine's Day. Yet nobody ever complained or blamed, just improved and pivoted in the knowing we operated for something far bigger than ourselves. I promise you once you have experienced the synergy and capabilities of an elite group working together, winning, losing, and learning as one, it changes everything.

Babysitting the rich and shameless and navigating the corporate toxicities to the extent I had, had long stopped feeling an honour and privilege, in fact it was now torture. Something was wrong. With me. The juice wasn't worth the squeeze for me anymore; worn down by the bullshit and lost without purpose. A challenge, or at least an iron to sharpen myself against. I was bored and lonely, so I started acting out of character as my discipline began to give way to frustration and fury. I began to get physically, and although I refused to admit it, mentally ill. I had been many people in my life, a chameleon, and a fucking great one because even I didn't know who I was anymore. Since entering the film security industry, I had been forced to operate against my values time and time again without support or justification; I had lost my purpose and hated being a cog in the bullshit I despised. Working with fickle and uninterested individuals who stood for nothing other than their own personal progression didn't compute. Slowly I alienated myself from my Royal Marine brothers and those who had served as a constant inspiration and guide to maintaining consistency of growth as I subconsciously worked to ignore the fact, I was devolving back to my original loser self. I became lost, sad, and ashamed. So much so, I doubled down in my personal devolution to convince myself I was just going through a phase and that this was the right thing for me and my future. But in this world, we have to be ourselves. Suppressing us will destroy us. And just as this conclusion began to unravel itself in my mind, the world fell to shit under the façade of Covid.

The world went to shit, and I discovered just how human I really was. In 2020 I was introduced to my mortality. The world was suffering, and I was suffering in silence. Locked away in my ivory tower of a beautiful Surrey home, with a southwest facing garden, a brand-new Mercedes on the driveway, and beautiful girlfriend; I could not have been more miserable! Suicide on my mind. I had achieved far more than I thought I would in such a short amount of time and for some reason I was bitter about it. I felt such a huge disconnect, watching the world tear itself apart as our freedoms were torn from us. It really scared and saddened me. I began to spin out of control and into depression with nothing to do in my spoilt life. Looking for trouble as lockdown set in, I began drinking and taking drugs. Even picking fights with the dealers for entertainment. What was wrong with me? Why was I so set on self-destruction? I should have been happy. I was blessed, compared to most. Adam had come to live with me which only made things worse as he had become extremely controlled by his girlfriend and changed an immense amount. He quite simply didn't care I was in a shit state but cared that his girlfriend was coming to stay at my home with us and how that would affect her. That one hurt. But men do the craziest things when they are in love and despite it all I was happy to see him in love after years of confessed loneliness. But at the time I felt I had lost another brother.

Then one early morning in August 2020 I received a phone call from Ryan's mum who was hysterical. I sat on the phone as she pulled herself together but knew. I was out the door and in my car ready to go but when she said the words, they landed so heavy upon my chest, it was like being shot with a shotgun. Crippling sadness. Ryan had been struggling with money and his baby mother weaponizing their child, my god daughter. We had spoken a lot recently and even Facetimed the day before, but when his mother told me he had taken his own life, I just went numb. I laughed in shock and then cried heavily and quietly so his mother wouldn't hear me. I hadn't cried in forever. I grabbed Lilo & Stitch and drove to his house on autopilot, I still don't remember the journey. When I arrived, I took care of what his mother had asked. To do that I had to go into Ryan's house, and I saw him lying there. I whispered my goodbyes and couldn't bring myself to read the note on the bedside cabinet. I had to leave so I could do what his mother asked. I left, did what I had to do and then went home. Taking cocaine as I drove home to numb my brain and the pain. I began to feel a rage. Protecting myself from sadness. My head was in a blender.

By the time I was home it was light. I couldn't tell anyone what had happened so didn't. I went back to bed and cuddled with Lilo and Stitch, like a child would cling to a parent when scared. I know how crazy this sounds and it was as sad a picture as it sounds. Pathetic even. I tried to talk to Adam, but I couldn't. He didn't understand and had not been able to help with the issues I was suffering with previously, seemingly missing the issue but then again, we had always had such a man's relationship, void of emotion, and this was a first for us both. He's a legend but has the emotional intelligence of a rock. A reason I love him and the reason we have always been so close. Because he never asked, and I never told.

Sitting alone again, it had already been three weeks since that night and months into the Covid induced frustration that had me bouncing around my house deep within myself as my mental health deteriorated. I became snappy and grumpy as I used anger to push people away and hide my pain. Things got so bad that I tried anti-depression medication, but they didn't help. They made me numb and I felt safer feeling the pain. I was spiralling and reaching out for a purpose in all the directions I shouldn't. Anything, I was desperate. I started taking different types of drugs to numb my mind, but you cannot fuck, drink, smoke or snort your problems away. Trust me, I tried, and it only makes things a whole lot worse.

I began undoing everything I had worked so hard to change about myself. My mothers mental state had been deteriorating for years and we had become distant as her ex-con loser boyfriend filled her head with nonsense and stole from her. You can imagine my reaction. Then I got myself into a very toxic relationship with someone who was of a very sheltered and privileged background; suffered from a physical illness and bi-polar disorder. I was trying to use two broken pieces to fix a puzzle again. She understandably had an overwhelming bitterness because of her illness but I didn't care, I loved her. I thought she was made for me and my need to be needed was filled to the brim. My need to be the fucking hero went into overdrive. I fell in love so deeply with her and the idea of us it was beyond words. She had all the money she needed so wanted me, didn't need me. She was a lady in the street and as wild as you like in bed. But we shared some tender moments I will never forget. Even if they were based on lies, they were true to me in those moments and in that moment, I had lost rationality. I left my professional and pragmatic brain way back down the road in a desperate attempt to find a Disney worthy happy ending. However, I soon found out she had lied about pretty much everything and gave me no choice but to accept she was full of shit like everyone around me had been telling me for months. I was heartbroken, embarrassed, and missed the vulnerability that only comes with love. A rare feeling for me. You cannot have a relationship with someone who holds others to a standard they do not hold themselves to. It will never last, and often these people are masters at acting the victim and will frame and create situations to judge you by your reaction to their disrespect. This is the definition of manipulation. I just couldn't believe it. How could I be so stupid!?! Why couldn't I see the signs?? Was I that blinded by a pretty face? Was I that desperate for love? I had been paid to profile people in extreme situations, but I couldn't see through the lies of someone so close to me. It is here for the first time that I really began to hate myself. My self-confidence and self-value dissolved.

The next day I had a huge opportunity, one dreams are made of and one I had worked very hard for. I pulled myself together like I had done so many times before. Pushing all my thoughts and feelings into that box so I could present myself as the professional I had to be. The opportunity was a huge meeting with Avalon Production company. I had pitched a TV show I had written based loosely on my life, and this was the meeting to define whether they would buy into my concept. They did, I got the offer I wanted. Selling my first TV Show, on my very first attempt. Well, the idea anyway. I should have been on cloud nine, but success is lonelier than failure and the only person I wanted to share it with was her, and I hated myself for it. I never hated her, just myself. I was consumed with sadness on a day that should have been one to remember. Instead of drinking to celebrate I began drinking to numb the pain. I drank and drank and drank. Messaging old friends nostalgic bullshit and remember-when's, desperate for a sign of life or love. Specifically messaging my brother from another as he hadn't answered my calls that day. Texting him sarcastically: 'Are your alive blood?'.

I woke up naked on my kitchen floor, my loyal little Lilo and Stitch cuddling up to me. It was around 9am; I felt like death. I stood up and stumbled to the fridge to start my recovery. I went into my front room and sat down, as I did so I got a WhatsApp from my mum, a fucking WhatsApp! 'I have some bad news. Jamie passed away last night'. Just like that... What a way to find out. I was crushed. I went numb... sat on my sofa, I couldn't think or function as shock set in. I called Adam and tried telling him what had happened, but I couldn't speak coherently. I hung up the phone and sat on my sofa and cried so hard my chest and eyes burnt. I was already desperate and now I had lost a brother who had been more of a brother to me than my own blood brothers. In my opinion a brother is a title earned, a sibling is a title given. My blood brothers couldn't tell you one thing they have ever done for me, but Jamie had always been there, as I was for him.

I have been through many challenges and loss in my life, but the last few weeks had left me a shadow of who I had become. This former cheeky chappy, Commando, Bodyguard, 007 wannabe turned entrepreneur devolved back into a scared and lonely little boy. I have never felt more alone or desperate in my life. Adam messaged my ex to tell her what had happened in the hope she would contact me to say a kind word or two. He knew I missed her and that a word from her despite it all would help. But she replied saying we should not speak as I had told her to stop calling me. Bitter at me for finishing our relationship whilst proving I was right to do so. She told Adam I hadn't wanted to talk to her before, so she didn't want to talk to me now. It was apparently a day for cuntish messages. I got in my car and drove to Enfield to see my friends. Taking a work call on the route and setting up a new job to start the following day. No matter my pain I felt comfort in the safety and predictability of work. Crying the second I hung up, feeling guilty for doing so. I saw some friends, and it made things worse. I felt more alienated and alone than before. Returning home alone that night as Lilo and Stitch were at home, and I hadn't wanted to take them with me.

I didn't really do anything for the next few days. I let Lilo and Stitch into the garden to use the bathroom but that was it. Only leaving the house for Ryan's funeral.

A few days later I was at home and decided it was time to put myself out of my misery. I had better friends waiting for me on the other side, why would I want to be here anymore. I went into my loft, got some cable, dropped Lilo and Stitch to my friend's house and drove to Richmond Park. I fucked off the idea of leaving a note, why? No one gave a shit whilst I was alive so why would they care if I was dead? It angered me at the thought of people crying at the news of my death when they had been so avoidant to helping me in life. I drove to Richmond Park and had decided to hang myself at my favourite sunset spot. I had to stop the pain; my mental pain had become physically crippling. I couldn't see the light and wanted to see my friends to tell them I was sorry. I believed this was the only way to stop the pain. But the universe had other plans that day. Music had automatically linked up from my phone and I had let it play. Now I wouldn't believe this if someone told me and I couldn't believe it at the time either, but just as I entered the park gates, the sun beginning to set, the cable noose on the passenger seat. The line from Dave's Psycho songs rang out and through me...

"If you're thinking 'bout doing it/Suicide doesn't stop the pain, you're only moving it/Lives that you're ruining/Thoughts of a world without you in it."

– Dave, Psycho, Psychodrama

I snatched at it, turning it off and punching my steering wheel, cutting my knuckles. The pain was a relief. I began a ferocious internal dialogue; a literal screaming match in my head about what I was about to do. Imagining my little sister and friends being told what I had done. Fuck Dave! fuck everyone, no one was there for me. I ran to where I was going before I could change my mind. I climbed the tree and tied it to a thick enough branch above the one I was sitting on. I had this planned in my head a long time ago. Sitting on the thicker branch below, a noose dangling next to me. As soon as I was in that position, I felt a wave of humility come over me. How could I do this to my loved ones, hand them my pain and step away like everyone I detested. I cried so hard that a woman and her husband walked over, calling as they came to see if I was ok. I quickly wrapped the rope around the branch, so it was kind of hidden and jumped down. I thanked them for caring and walked off to my car without explanation.

Now what... Can you imagine my drive home? Obviously, no music was played as I slowly drove home.

Back home with Lilo & Stitch, laying in the foetal position and fell to sleep, I was exhausted.

The next day I reached out to family and friends for help. But everyone was struggling. "We are all going through hard times Craig, come on, you're stronger than this." So, I shrunk back into my shell and weathered the storm. The guilt that I had been protecting so many people I didn't know but couldn't protect my closest friends. I was emotionally vacant at this point. Numb. Lost at best and spiralling with drug dealers and shit food my only interactions of the day. I locked myself away with the dogs and drank morning to night and smoked enough weed to cater for a Rastafarian wedding. Mornings were the worst as I would cry in my sleep and wake up exhausted and miserable. I just wanted to die; I wasn't interested in anything. I cried every morning for weeks as the flood gates opened, and I vented as if I had been waiting a century for this moment. I felt broken, my mind constantly overwhelmed and numb as I grieved, delt with heart break, and recognised, no, obsessed over every fuck up I had ever made. Torturing myself as I fought not to go back to Richmond Park; only this time I would turn the fucking music off. I was either crying with awkward vulnerability or furious and wanting all the smoke. I began going out into the streets to find groups of men to fight with and when that didn't work, I would call drug dealers to my house and batter them unconscious before robbing them and driving them in their own car a few streets away before going back to my house and waiting almost joyfully for their retaliation that never came. My self-destruct mode was fully engaged as the grief and embarrassment of my last relationship tore through me and I just wanted to die. My mind telling me I was a victim and suffering because the world was against me. The truth is the world didn't care either way. Too busy with its own problems and bullshit to worry itself about my insignificance.

Our mind is not our friend, we need to feed it positive things about ourselves, or risk losing the battle within and subsequently lose the war within, let alone the war with the outside world. Because before anything is possible, we must truly know who we are and trust ourselves. I didn't even know who I was.

I was reading one day and came across the African Proverb: "If there is no enemy within, the enemy outside cannot harm us." Well, the enemy was living in my head rent free. I had truly lost my mind in relation to all those around me who defended their comfort zones socially dictated lifestyles, even at the cost of living a known lie and life of silent desperation. However, 'losing our mind' is simply losing the construct of self, the old us, a recognition that we didn't have it all figured out. Once accepted, we are free to nurture ourselves into the person we wish to become. Relinquishing control and socially dictated constraints to apply extreme ownership upon us. Everyone is capable of overcoming adversity, but not without belief or self-value. I had lost both.

I recognized how lost I was and how much of it was my fault. I had lost accountability to myself and knew I was all alone on this path and had to get busy living or I should get busy dying to maintain the public persona of my professional self. I didn't want the last memories of me to be a dribbling mess, no matter the circumstance. I then made the best decision I have ever made for myself. I switched off my phone and spent a week with Lilo and Stitch on epic walks and thinking about what I really wanted from life. No one had put a gun to my head so I had made all the choices that got me into this state, and I could get myself out. However, at the time I just let it all out. From fighting trees and screaming at the top of my lunges to crying in a puppy cuddle under trees as it rained.

260

I have never been more humbled or low in my life. I felt unworthy of even my dogs love. My head was fucked! Finally, with the support of Juniour, I finally accepted that I needed professional help. I went to the NHS and was put on their watch list. But no one ever called or helped. I then privately saw two psychologists, they were terrible. Book smart with no life experience. I ended up helping them as I used my skillset to turn the conversation onto them. I still have emails from them both thanking me for helping them. I fell deeper into loneliness. I slowly became void of caring and wanted out. I decided I would go to visit my mum to say goodbye and then return to my favorite tree.

I hadn't seen her in around 18 months but when I arrived, she had changed. She took a picture of me as I left the airport without me knowing and posted in on Facebook saying I had come to look after her. I looked like a crackhead and was furious she would do and say these things, especially online, especially right now. She wasn't herself and had sadly become more ill. Showing serious signs of dementia. She picked fights with me from the moment I arrived, and I knew she was hiding something. It was how she had always acted when she had done something she knew was wrong but was about to double down on it and cause issues. I knew her so well as she not only watched me learn to lie but I grew up watching her lie too. Her boyfriend had convinced her to sign over half of her retirement home to him. She was also hiding the fact my sibling was getting married for some reason. I thought this was all strange and uncalled for. She hadn't asked how I was or anything. She was volatile towards me like I had done something wrong. She told me I was being ridiculous when asked what was going on, so I just thought I was just being needy in my vulnerable state and left it. Our relationship had fractured over the years after she began dating this guy who used to steal off elderly clients when working in their homes and show off about it; then my middle sibling stole a little under £8,500 from me and I was asked to just forget it and move on. I couldn't, so things had been rough as it was me who was punished. I was never a fan of my sibling as he is the type of guy who shows off about cheating on his wife, sending me pictures of other women in his bed as he tried to compete with me on every level available to him. We had had to ban talking about the Marines or my adventures at home years ago because he turned viciously jealous. Even after I got him a job and accommodation in Spain. But I understand this, anyone who cheats on their partner will cheat on you as a friend. You are either loyal or disloyal, as I have mentioned before. The only difference being is that we make excuses and justify, to remove accountability for those closest to us. We all do it so we don't end up alone but it is this double edged sword that makes success a lonely journey.

I arrived and was so excited to see my mum, I had always been a mamma's boy as you know, and had missed her badly. But she was different. She told me she would be popping out the following day for lunch with her friend, it was his birthday, and she didn't want to miss it. I was stunned. I was her first born and visibly looked depressed, but she didn't seem to care. I said OK. However, I woke up at 0900 the following morning and she was already gone and didn't return until 1900 that night. I couldn't believe it. She lives in a very remote area where you need to have a car to go anywhere. She had left me all that time when I was extremely suicidal. Her friends messaging me well wishes and support as it was no longer a secret, but she had left me alone. My head started to go as I sat stunned in her front room, I called her, no answer. Fuck! I had to stay busy. I went around her house and cleaned the horrendous mess, literal filth under the sofa and everywhere other than in plain sight. Clearly no one had been helping her. I then went into the garden and scoped the entire property. I then went running and by the time she got home I was in clear distress. She came in and I asked her why she was gone so long. She said she had asked me and claimed not to understand what my issue was. I then told her I had sorted all of the garden and she turned, looked me in my eye and said, "there is a stain on the toilet too, you can do that if you like". I lost it. "What happened to you? You were my hero and now look at you, talk about show me your friends and I'll show you your future." She turned, walked into her bedroom, slammed the door, and shouted, "miserable prick". I was crushed. Not now, I needed my mum, and she was clearly gone. Lost to her illness and the cunts around her. I raged in the room I was staying in until she suddenly walked in and threw a little piece of paper with the Samaritan name and number on it. I raged! I've been on the suicide watch list for fucking months, what are you talking about!". She went back to her room.

The following day I was a sorry sight and was meant to borrow her car to visit a friend, but again when I woke, she had learnt it to the same friend she left me for the day before. I was so angry I grabbed my electric scooter and missioned 40 minutes to the station before getting the train into town. I got some weed and drank to numb myself. I was devastated and thinking of that beautiful sunset tree that could take it all away. I had lost myself and all my value by this point. I wanted to die. Then, like a sign from heaven, I received an email from Avalon Production asking me to meet the producer in London in a couple of days. Our first in-person meeting. That email stopped me from doing something very silly. I got on that plane back to the UK even worse than when I had left.

I met the EMMY winning producer James Taylor looking like complete shit, eyes puffy from the stress, I presented myself terribly as my focus was all over the place; but James was great, and we spoke through everything. Well, nearly everything, I didn't want to scare him off. I went home and wrote and wrote and wrote; this book primarily, but also multiple scripts and anything I could to keep me occupied. I decided right there and then I wasn't going anywhere. I was going to go for my dream. It was now or never. Actor, writer, producer, who cares. I wanted to express myself and help people. If I could help just one person, then it would all be worth it. I had always wanted to start bootcamps and decided I would do that too. I could use my pain to empower others. I became obsessed! I put all my pain on the page and started to work out and eat again. I had dropped from 94kgs+ to 72kgs and looked like a crack head. I had been cutting the sides of my hair out of distress. I was a podgy-skinny mess, but the mental pain had gotten so bad I was lost to others perception of me. I just didn't care, I had no pride or self-value left.

I got put in touch with an incredible therapist and human being I am not allowed to mention by name, but he saved me. We had three sessions and he stripped back all the bullshit until I was raw with emotion and things literally began to make sense to me again. He explained I wasn't like other people and had been elevated to a mental state through my experiences and through my suffering that most would never understand. That by trying to reintegrate by acting like normal people I had torn at my very fabric and lost myself just like most people do every single day. Lying to themselves and hiding in their comfort zones, lying to themselves over and over until they believed their own bullshit. He recognized that most of my trauma came from losing Jay at such a young age and the role I had within my household. Such pressure for a young man and I had bottled it up for years. My is ambition a vehicle to find self-value and appreciation, however this would be a cup that would never fill as I would never be good enough for me. He was so right about it so much I felt better after our first session. We then came onto my mother who I viciously protected against his suggestions that she had manipulated me into being her protector. What??? I was her son and that was my duty. But as he broke it down and explained he wasn't shitting on my mother but was explaining the pressures in relation to me and the accountabilities surrounding the situation at the time. It isn't all right and wrong, black and white, the world is mostly an off grey area and he wanted to shine light on it for me. He would hand me the tools, but it was up to me to use them.

He got me to put a list together to talk to my mum about all the things that were weighing on me so. I called my mum one night and went through the list but not so she would not. Confiding in her. Telling her truths about her boyfriend stealing from her, stealing from elderly clients, and manipulating her. Asking why she treated me differently to my brothers and why she supported my middle brother who had stollen nearly £8,500 from me and cheated on his fiancée and everyone know, just as she did but she did and said nothing yet treated me so harshly. Her answer, she had to protect them from me. Me! I hung up and cried myself to sleep but things would get worse. When she hung up, she called everyone I knew in Spain and the UK and spread the word that I had vowed to ruin my sibling's wedding. I wouldn't find out she had done this until months later and it crushed me. I was drowning and she had thrown me two anchors. The mother I knew was lost to mental illness and manipulation by those who should have been looking after her. But either way she was lost to me, and I had to move on. This remains the hardest thing I have ever had to deal with in my life. Losing my relationship with my mother, especially at this point in my life, cut me to my soul and I have tears running down my cheeks as I write this now.

This set me on a path to challenge every relationship I had. I spiraled further as I searched for who I was and who I had around me. I decided to sell my house, car, and liquidate my company. I moved to Barcelona to be alone with Lilo and Stitch. I needed space to breathe and recover.

In Barcelona I began to rebuild myself. Taking full accountability and without distractions I quickly went from strength to strength. In hindsight this was the best thing I could do for myself. Removing victimisation and toxicity from my mental. I evolved into the person I had to be to achieve what I had, but how could I expect to maintain those mindsets when surrounding myself with people who didn't understand these mindsets? Even attacking them and their requirements whilst enjoying the benefits they brought through my application of hard work and dedication. I went right back to the start and began writing obsessively, trying to figure out a path back to the me who understood mindset was everything. I started again, getting up at 0600, no matter my state from the night before. I got my ass out of bed and did something. I got up and got moving. Walked the dogs, cleaned the house, anything, I just got up! It was the hardest part of my day. I woke up in bits each and every day but slowly but surely it got a little easier. I had to learn who I was and how to become who I wanted to be. Sometimes getting lost is the best way to find yourself. I stopped screaming and punishing myself with drugs and began a purposeful dialogue with myself. Going for long walks with my headphones on to act if I were on a telephone call. But the conversation I was having didn't have anything to do with anyone else. I would walk and talk myself through my story. Reminding myself how far I had come and the endless blessings of adventure and experiences I had, had. This book began from those notes. Notes I was using to help build a new me. A new process and life for myself.

I began purposely manifesting again. Looking in the mirror and talking with myself as if I was my own best friend. When you look at yourself in moments like this you see your own pain. You see yourself as a human, someone who needs love and support, not to be kicked whilst they're down. I had been beating myself up for months and finally began to be nice to myself.

Manifesting out loud. I wanted to build a road to recovery that would keep me consistently focused on my goals. A light leading me back to their path of choice but one that would empower them to not just heal but grow back into the best version of myself. My drive and purpose started to return as I knew my absent friends were watching. I knew I didn't want to go back to protecting people I only professionally cared about and knew I could help people from across the world who really needed help overcoming mental health and managing the overwhelming bullshit of the world to become versions of themselves they never thought possible. I had helped clients and friends do this for years so knew if I could build an elite roadmap to success to get me out of the darkness and save myself. I could help others dominate their lives. I woke up every morning and played songs as I bounced to my morning affirmation – "Make money, help people. Make money, help people. Make money, help people". Over and over for fiver repeats of the song Luv 2 U. Walker, Roxi Yung.

I broke down everything I admired and what I wanted to bring with me from my old self into the new ultimate version of Craig Ainsworth. A strong mind and a soft heart. A true Alpha who created safe spaces and unity. Where virtue was protected by savagery. That was it! I created Virtuous Savage, a course to help people become the very best versions of themselves. No matter who we are or what status we hold in life, it is always you vs you and we are each our own superhero and villain, as I taught people this, I reminded myself of these facts and so a positive snowball effect began. Supported by an ethos to empower consistency, the ALPHA mindset. Accountability, Lessons not losses, Positivity, Humility, & Action. I used this to drive myself each day into an empowered mindset built upon actions I knew would bare results. Looking after myself. Focusing on me. My mind and body became president over everything. If I had a bad day, I would chill. I came first.

I meditated, took breathing classes, yoga, MMA, I started enjoying myself again. Remembering all the experience and all the tools I had gathered along the way and how I could help people become the best versions of themselves. I used my programs and rituals like output mornings and input evenings instrumental to my renewed energy to build a program that could be taught to others. I had managed to fight my way to the top of the industry I had attempted to be a part of and now I had a genuine goal that could help not only the ultra-wealthy and famous, but everyone to take control of their lives. I sat and reflected long enough. It was time to get back to the pursuit of excellence but this time I would blaze my own path. I quickly became addicted to my secret world. I started being able to look at myself in the mirror again. I began training and even dating. No matter where I was, I would get up at 5am. Write. Vocalise. Manifesting before the sun rose. I would walk the dogs around beautiful Barcelona, ending up at the beach gym bars each morning where the fur babies would chill out whilst I trained. My body was in bits as I had abused it. My mind was still weaker but as my dedication grew so did my mind and body's resilience. I began to feel empowered and angry again. Angry I had dared to forget my greatness and the sufferings I had been through, how dare I let the world beat me into submission. A whirlwind of emotion started to drive my discipline. I was at war with the world but if I could win the battle with myself that would be enough. I decided if I could help just one person suffering as I had it would be worth it so that was my goal. If I could fall into such a mindset with all my training and life experience, I could only imagine how hard others were finding life. That was my reason. My purpose. I had lost accountability for myself, those around me, and my environment. No excuses. It is a superpower to even admit that. In modern western culture accountability is often perceived as taking a position of guilt, or blame. Rubbish! It is freeing and the core of disciplined and structured growth all successful people follow in one form or another.

By taking accountability of my time, actions, and words I was able to discover who I really was again. Lost, residing in a manicured comfort zone I had worked so hard for, but the juice just wasn't worth the squeeze. It was the comradery and challenge I missed and subconsciously sought. However, billionaires were often very lonely. Celebrities missed their little freedoms. Soldiers missed their families. I realised that everybody had so much in common, struggling with the same issues no matter their wealth, status, race, religion, or geographical location. Human. A human has needs, essentials in which it needs to survive, and we all place other people at the very top of that. It is each other. Being poor is when you have enough but need more. Humble gratitude and suffering made me thankful for the positives considering the dark times. I had lived through madness and asked for more but managed to keep a soft heart despite my fierce head. Because I didn't fucking care anymore, I worked week because I wasn't worried about failure. I literally didn't care, so I was relaxed and therefore the process was too. Barcelona was now home but I needed to spread my wings a little further; so, I started with Mexico, then Morocco, Bali, Peru, Colombia, Africa, Dubai, and a European road trip with Lilo & Stitch. France, Switzerland, Italy, Spain, and Portugal. My favourite things about life are traveling, meeting new people, and learning about new cultures. Your mindset is forever feasting on diversity, and you are made aware of who you really are. I have learnt so much from strangers I met and was gifted from a young age being immersed in cultures from around the globe. Good old north London I grew up with Africans, Jamaicans, Indians, Pakistanis, Bengalis, Arabs, Asians, Everyone! London is the most diverse city in the world and that was a gift for me

I never appreciated until I got into business and was put into intense situations. My natural acceptance and inclusion of other cultures, ideas and beliefs had made me tolerant of others' ideas, even if they contradicted my own. I have protected the Aga Khan and an Israeli Government official in the same week. People are people and I judge people by their actions. Both men were great and kind men, I put my life before theirs as duty. To have friends who challenge your beliefs is a gift. The best thing that ever happened to me was spending time with Arabic royalty at the polo or surrounded by VIP celebrities at the best party in town so I could learn just how human we all are, and everyone becomes familiar with their lifestyle, so our privileges become the norm. We become ungrateful. Lost as to why we are doing whatever we are doing when we have all the shit, we need but still feel empty. The answer across the board has been each other. Family, friendships, time, and presence. No matter what you achieve in life you will always be you. You should live your life for the right reasons or no matter what you achieve it will always be tainted. The juice that wasn't worth the squeeze. Money and fame don't solve problems it enables bigger ones. The good thing is we get to choose the version of that person we create despite of life's trials and tribulations.

I can put myself in a headspace where I remember exactly how it feels to be utterly depressed. Thinking back to things I have written about in this book makes my chest tight with emotion and I have shed a tear or two. But I have had such an amazing life full of adventure. The juice was worth the squeeze, and I have tried to take strength from the losses, but it's been rough for some days. I have found that by sharing what I have been through has brought so many people closer to me. Clients have become friends and even asked me to coach them or family members privately as I understood the sensitivities, but also that my experiences and achievements mean something to the UHNWs and competitors I had previously provided security services to. Coaching came naturally to me as I have always taken a no bullshit approach that bears fruit from people no matter their situation. It's all about my journey and my relationship with self. It's been awesome to see how some fun workshops can bring people into their own. It has genuinely given me purpose. Seeing people start to believe in themselves is beautiful. We are so similar but so different and to see some cry, some laugh, others get furious, and it is never who you think. You watch one of my lady legends realise she's her own hero and villain, accountable to her boundaries and comfortable with who she is. Beast! Don't mess with her. I told you, forget the bodybuilder Alpha concept because western society has evolved overtime with the many privileges, we all benefit from, rendering us spoilt in many ways compared to the rest of the world. Violence and corruption plague many of the world's societies but in the west, we have the freedom to be anything we dream of. Supported by this system. It's all about mindset and culture these days people, the only inequality in equality being belief and effort. If 50 Cent and Nadia Nadim can do it, so can you.

I spent months locked away from the world, writing and taking influence from people's stories I had met or read about as I sought positive influence from the world. I had been consumed by what I had focussed on. Threats and the negatives of the world; I had always known that we become what we focus on, however consciously I had been focussing on problem solving and protection, whilst subconsciously I had been absorbing the stress and fear without processing it, I simply ignored that stuff. A solid tactic. Like a pressure pot, it had built and built as the stress became normalised, as did the version of me I created to manage. We are powerful beyond measure when our mind, body and soul are in synergy. To control and maintain this focus and power is the definition of excellence but we are all human no matter how hard we work to ignore it.

I had taken time for me and learnt who I was. Who I had been and everything in between. It was so hard at times, I thought I was going crazy. Maybe I was, maybe I am. But I knew I could help people with my story and the lessons I had learnt along the way. I soon realised men would listen and open up to me because I presented the definition of an alpha male on paper, and my openness would pave the way for others to feel safe to speak about their feelings so we could grow from it, bigger, better, stronger. A fierce mind and soft heart.

When I was at my worst. I was so lost to everything and felt like I was broken. Pushing away everyone I loved with needless insecurity driven tests or ignoring them altogether. Furious at the world for what it had done to me. A true mess and doing all the bad things. By taking control and not giving up I managed to get through it. I'm never over it but I certainly went through it. Now I enjoy coaching people and taking them on expeditions to show them their full potential and the mindset they can tap into. Investing in their inner hero and supporting them to build the confidence to tap into their intuition and live purposely. The satisfaction I get in taking my clients through the process is unrivalled. Watching people outdo themselves and grow into themselves as they get out of their own way and invest in their hero, battling their villain with self-love. I sound mental don't I. But if you have all the answers you just need to be taken out of your comfort zone and reinvigorated and we restructure you a little. That's literally what I did over months to pull myself back and now I use it to help people build them they want.

I realised that my experiences had taken me to places and shown me so much about so many secret worlds that my perspective on many things would always be different from others. I have accepted that I am different, and that loneliness motivates me into my disciplined processes to achieve and gain recognition from the very people I ran from. Fuelling my audacious and fearless pursuit of my limits. Running up volcanoes in Bali or cutting my way through the Colombian jungle; even getting caught up in the Peruvian riots on my birthday of all things; I love it and it brought the best in me as I felt alive again. Creating Virtuous Savage and coaching has allowed me to share so much with my client s but has rewarded me with so much more. So, as I come to the end of this book and the first 40 years of my life, I want to leave you with this...

Live fearlessly, fully aware that life is a precious and fleeting gift. Love fearlessly, without expecting anything in return. If something makes you happy, it doesn't have to make sense to others. Believe in yourself! You have to believe in you, only then will you have the courage to be true to who you are and build the best version of yourself. It's all on you.

Don't merely exist; live your life on your own terms. Most people simply go through the motions. Fame, wealth, and success all come with sacrifices, so make sure the juice is worth the squeeze. Bitterness arises when the trade-off doesn't measure up, so invest your time wisely. Remember that not everyone is watching you, and that you will only be criticised by someone by someone threatened by you. So let their insecurities fuel your dream.

Genuine tolerance is a superpower, and we can learn from everyone and everything. Especially those we might consider adversaries or enemies. Beware of fools, they have all the answers. Choose your company carefully.

We all make mistakes, so take ownership of yours. Forgive others once, but trust yourself above all else. Life is short, and we often depart without the chance to bid farewell. Therefore, seize every opportunity to express love to those around you—friends, siblings, parents—making sure they feel heard and valued. The most remarkable individuals I've encountered, both male and female, always do. We are all on this journey together, even though each of us ultimately faces it alone. Let's strive to make each other's existence a beautiful and fulfilling experience.

I have been blessed with a life of adventure and experienced so much and I am only 39 years old as I write this. I am starting a whole new chapter in my life dedicated to helping people realise you can achieve anything in this world when you truly dedicate yourself completely, no excuses, and it is now my life goal to show people just how great they can be when they get over their own bullshit. I hate the term "get over it" as we never get over things, we go through them and either take the lesson, or carry the bitter pain. Too many people suffer in silence and if this book or Virtuous Savage helps just person, I will die a happy man.

Visit Virtuous Savage at www.virtuoussavage.com or on our social medias @virtuoussavage

Remember. Life is an adventure, act accordingly...

Acknowledgments

In the pages of this book, I've poured my heart and soul, but it wouldn't have been possible without the unwavering support and inspiration from those who touched my life in profound ways.

First and foremost, I owe an immeasurable debt of gratitude to Juniour. In my darkest moments, he appeared as a beacon of light, reminding me that there could be hope even in the bleakest of times. His time, presence, and boundless support were the foundations upon which this book was built. Juniour, a man who's faced trials that would break most, yet chooses to radiate love and support with his enormous heart. His story is one of resilience, and I am eternally grateful for his friendship. May everyone be blessed with a Juniour in their lives.

To my mother, who demonstrated that even when life has you backed into a corner, you can still find a way. Regardless of gender or circumstance, the world has a knack for throwing challenges our way each morning to surpass yesterdays, and witnessing her struggle made me become the man I needed to be for you, and then myself. Her example taught me to greet those challenges with the ferocity they dictate but with a smile on your face and a dedication to maintaining a soft heart and tolerance for good, empowering you to keep pushing forward towards my ultimate goals and responsibilities.

My profound gratitude extends to the Royal Marines, whose teachings instilled in me self-worth, accountability, and the invaluable Commando mindset. This mindset has been my guiding star, enabling me to become the best version of myself, even as I grapple with my inner demons daily, not to mention others fears and ignorance's.

Sonia Amin, my Barcelona legend and for sure lifelong friend, deserves a special mention. Throughout the writing of this book, as I revisited the trauma, pain, and strain of my life, her unwavering support, kind words, and presence were my lifeline on days when I battled with despair and suicidal thoughts. She is my Barcelona hero, and I am forever grateful.

Ishkiran, a true legend in every sense, showed me that people can indeed be everything they claim to be and more. Her consistent support and her approach to life's challenges with an open heart and mind have been a wellspring of inspiration. Her beautiful soul has rekindled my faith in the existence of genuinely good people.

To all my clients and those who encouraged me to share my story in its unvarnished truth, I extend my heartfelt appreciation. And to my haters and challengers, you played a crucial role in pushing me forward. Without adversity and opposition, I might never have embarked on this journey.

Lastly, I want to acknowledge myself. For finding the courage to fight back when all seemed lost. I've faced many battles in my life, but the one against suicidal thoughts, grief, and depression was a harrowing one. It's a battle I wouldn't wish upon anyone, and I pledge to spend the rest of my days alleviating the suffering of others. I was at my lowest point, enduring the excruciating mental pain that manifested physically, but I persevered. I thank the universe for this humbling lesson, and as I conclude these words, I invite you all to join me on my Virtuous Savage journey. Together, we'll confront the battles within our minds and discover the greatness that resides within when and show you how great you truly are when you get out of your own way.

Printed in Great Britain
by Amazon

31248791R00159